Full Color Living™

*Transform your life
from simply surviving
to absolutely thriving!*

Jennifer Joy Walker

Full Color Living™

*Transform your life
from simply surviving
to absolutely thriving!*

Copyright ©2009 by Jennifer Joy Walker
Printed in the United States of America
All rights reserved.

Library of Congress Cataloging-in-Publication Data
Walker, Jennifer Joy
Full color living: transform your life from simply surviving to absolutely thriving!/ Jennifer Joy Walker - 1st ed.
ISBN 1-4392-1285-6
Library of Congress Control Number 2008909535

DEDICATION

In loving memory of my dear parents,

Mickey Walker,
who loved good jazz, sailing,
and his bustling, cosmopolitan hometown of
Vancouver, B.C.

and

Lillie Holeksa Beharry,
who loved classical music, gardening,
and the peaceful vistas of her native Canadian prairie.

The authentic self is the soul made visible.
  Sarah Ban Breathnach

CONTENTS

	Introduction	7
	WHO IS *MYSELF*?	
one	Listening to the Inner Voice	15
two	Finding the Center	20
three	The Inner Committee	26
four	Conditions for Full Color Living	32
five	Full Color Emotions	42
	HOW TO BE TRUE	
six	Disciplines of Full Color Living	52
seven	Full Color Perspective	62
eight	Clues to Full Color Living	75
nine	The Promise of Surrender	99
ten	Barriers to Full Color Living	107
eleven	Nurturing a Full Color Life	115
twelve	Full Color Relationships	123
	EXPRESSION	
thirteen	Full Color Living	134
	About the Author	145
	Bibliography & Resources	146
	References	149

ACKNOWLEDGMENTS

Thank you to all my interview subjects, for your wisdom, wonderful stories, enthusiasm and support.

To friends and colleagues who helped by reading the manuscript, recommending resources, and keeping me focused. Special thanks to Betsy Kleiman — a true companion on the way.

To Thomas Yeomans, Ph.D., a gifted teacher and practitioner of spiritual psychology, who tremendously influenced my thinking.

To speaker and author Rosita Perez, whose life and message inspired others to full color living.

To my Walker family — Stella, Stuart, Laurel and Stephanie — for your laughter and good company on the journey.

To Cooper, Kate, and Carly — blessings in my life.

Finally, my gratitude to my dear husband, Woody Fletcher, for encouraging me to take a sabbatical, not knowing it would result in a book!

INTRODUCTION

The glory of God is a person fully alive!
St. Irenaeus

Why is it that some people are living lives that are authentic, satisfying, even passionate and jubilant — and others aren't?

Why does one person practically glow with the joy of the day's activities, while the other drags herself through her day?

Why do we look around ourselves in our day-to-day world and see so many people living gray existences, worn out and discouraged by the stress and cares of their lives?

More importantly, <u>what is the secret of those who are thriving</u>, even in similar circumstances?

Wouldn't it be great to have the answer to this question?

You do, here in this book.

This topic — how can we move from simply surviving to absolutely thriving — has always fascinated me. We each have the desire and capacity to fulfill our potential and

our dreams — in short, to fully embody our lives. But too often, people limit themselves, living in shades of gray instead of expressing themselves in luminous color.

How can we, each of us, throw off these limitations and live a full color life right now? This vital question is the focus of the book. In it you will find a wide range of voices — not just mine, but those of people who are addressing the same challenges you are, and also writers who have wrestled with this question in different forms over the centuries.

Whether you have lived too long in shades of gray, or you are the kind of person who is always seeking new ways of understanding yourself so that you can live more fully, I hope you will join me in this journey.

WHAT IS FULL COLOR LIVING?

So what is 'full color living,' exactly? These three words capture my way of describing a fully embodied life, but it's a metaphor, not a definition. You might wonder,

> "Does it have to do with having a great job, or a happy relationship?"
> "Does it mean being successful?"
> "Does it require being high-energy and outgoing?"
> "Is it something I'd even *want*?!"

As part of researching this book, I asked my interviewees what they considered to be full color living. Here are a few of their definitions — see if they resonate with you:

> "I call it being authentically, creatively, joyfully self-expressed and inspired." -Megha

> "You feel alive, engaged with life. You feel vibrant. The lights are on and there's a certain full pastiche of emotion available from joy to deep sorrow. You allow yourself to be touched by life. It's not just joy and happiness, it's the full range." -Keith

> "As I look at it, full color living is really being true to yourself." -Jill

"For me it needs to include a vision I want to reach for and accomplish." -Michael

"I don't think it has to involve a big, bold, extroverted life. To me it has to do with balance and taking time to smell the multicolored roses." -Lanie

"Being fully alive is not always bright and shiny, never doing anything wrong. Full color living also involves embracing and letting yourself accept darkness and gray times." -Peter

"It's a sense of being comfortable in your own skin. It's a kind of joy. That's kind of a funny word but I think that's really it. I don't think you can truly inhabit your life and live it fully unless there is a sense of joy about it." -Sue

This last comment, "it's a kind of joy," captures for me the essence of full color living. As we go on, you'll discover how you can claim this joy and create your full color life.

THE PROCESS OF WRITING THE BOOK

They say you teach what you need to learn about. I think it is also true that we write about things we need to make our own.

The topic of 'full color living' has been on my mind for years. Ever since I first entered the world of work, I've wondered how I could help people move out of their semi-satisfying gray existences into more fully expressive and rewarding lives. I went back to school for a master's degree in vocational counseling and spiritual psychology. I worked with hundreds of clients as a career counselor, and later with organizations, exploring the question of how to support people in full color living. I'd often thought about writing something on this topic which I care about so passionately, but I never got started. Nevertheless, the idea quietly percolated.

One day, while driving to meet two of my good friends for lunch, a thought attacked me. It came from out of the blue and pounced: "Base it on interviews. Talk to people. You love to interview people. Let them guide you."

Tears came to my eyes. It was such a hit of inspiration. *Yes!* Rather than try to create my own personal treatise of how to live a fully self-expressive life, let me ask others. Let me be open to surprise. And that is what I did.

So where do you begin in identifying the right people to interview for a book like this? I began with my own unofficial criteria — that full color living includes being happy or satisfied with life, being actively engaged in life, and being authentic to one's individual identity.

I realized pretty quickly that it would be difficult to find people who are complete exemplars of full color living. Who can live a fully satisfying and self-expressive existence in all areas of life at all times? Probably no one. I wanted to talk with people who were actively engaged in figuring out how to live a life that for them was fulfilling and self-expressive. Even if they had aspects of life that were gray, they were working on it!

In response to an email sent out to a long list of friends, colleagues and other acquaintances, I was directed to a number of potential interviewees. I also had in mind others who would be great subjects. This was not a scientific process, and I didn't amass a huge database of responses. But in time, after dozens of interviews, several obviously recurring themes made themselves known, and I have built this book around them.

I wanted the interview process itself to be of value to my subjects. Not often do we have the chance to talk about how to make a life more meaningful and satisfying. Regularly, when I checked in at the end of the interview, I would hear that they had found it to be an uncommon and valuable conversation. One interviewee emailed me: "I keep coming back to our conversation in my mind. It was helpful for me to hear myself. Thanks again."

With every step of this project, I became less controlling, having more faith that what needed to emerge would. This held true for the questions. I started with a two-page questionnaire and pretty quickly had whittled it down to just three basic questions:

1. What does 'full color living' mean to you — how would you define or describe it?
2. What has been your experience in working toward a full color life? What have been the challenges? Learnings?
3. What advice do you have for the reader, someone who wants to live a full color life?

Soon I discovered that each person would bring a distinctive piece to the puzzle. Our conversations were free-ranging, and each person tended to focus on one or two key aspects of full color living — something they'd learned as a result of their own life experience. I grew to enjoy the sense of anticipation before each interview, not knowing where the light would shine.

Doing the interviews made the process of writing the book truly a gift to myself — I found the conversations full of wisdom and humanity. Several times I had the chance to reconnect with someone I'd known years earlier, which made the experience even richer.

The interviews guided the focus of the book. As someone with a background in career counseling and a life-long fascination with the concept of 'vocation,' I assumed that when speaking with people about full color living, I'd hear a lot about their activities — the ways in which they expressed themselves in the world.

I did hear some of that. But, overwhelmingly, rather than focusing on the 'doing' of their lives, they talked to me about their 'being.' They guided me to a conversation about the underpinnings or the inner workings of this life of self-expression. In other words, without an understanding and acceptance of the world within, self-expression in the outside world is hard indeed.

So the book isn't specifically about work, or vocation, or success or even activity. You'll see that we'll be covering many topics that might come under the heading of being, such as self-awareness, presence, and authenticity. These, and others, are the prerequisites to a self-expressive life.

Besides the voices of my interview subjects, you'll notice I've included many others — people whose books I've read and whose teachings I've valued over the years.

I hope *Full Color Living* — the book — will be a blessing to you. And that full color living — the life — is your destiny.

TO THE READER

As you read this book, let it disrupt your current thinking and assumptions, and entice you to consider something new — something that might inspire you to make a change or decision that will allow you to live a more fully expressed life.

Throughout the book, you will find opportunities for FULL COLOR REFLECTION. These exercises are designed to help you apply the principles of full color living to your own life. I suggest you keep a notebook at your side as you read, capturing your responses in it each time you are prompted with a FULL COLOR REFLECTION exercise. Doing the exercises will invest the material with your own wisdom and experience, and help you gain clarity about how to create your fully self-expressive life.

Finally, I encourage you to read this book actively — grab a pen and mark it up, underline, and write comments as we go. This will further encourage your active participation in the book. As a helpful byproduct, when you go back to it in a few years' time, you'll easily find the parts that were most meaningful to you.

Pen and notebook at hand? Let's begin!

WHO IS *MYSELF*?

one

LISTENING TO
THE INNER VOICE

Twenty years ago, I attended a three-day workshop on the topic of empowerment. This workshop was given by Gail Straub and David Gershon, two leaders in the field, and it was an intense, rich experience.

Over the course of the weekend, we did exercises alone or with a partner, and then gathered into small groups to discuss our experiences. One of the participants was a freelance writer from Brooklyn named Marcia.

It happened that several times Marcia and I ended up in the same small group. The first time, she explained to the group that she had recently been in Florida where she had a transforming experience swimming with dolphins. She assumed that was why her image in the exercise we had just completed was all about dolphins. We discussed it.

The second time I was in her small group, Marcia said, "It seems crazy, but the image that came to me this time also involved dolphins." And we discussed it.

Later we found ourselves together in a small group once more, and again she talked about dolphins. And again we discussed it.

On the last day, in our last meeting, I found myself yet again in a small group with Marcia. Our task had been to do a visualization exercise about how we would apply the approach we'd been studying to our future work. When it was her turn to speak, Marcia said, "I'm sure it's a metaphor for something, but my visualization was all about dolphins."

That could have been. Perhaps it was a metaphor. Yet I was moved to say, "Is it possible that your interest in dolphins isn't just a metaphor? Is it possible you want your work to include them in some way?" Tears flooded her cheeks, and she said she couldn't even bear to consider that possibility. Her desire was so strong, she couldn't allow herself to hope.

Others in the group chimed in, and eventually Marcia agreed to take two steps to explore her love of dolphins. One was very simple: find a poster of dolphins and put it over her computer, where she could see it as she worked. The other was to find out whether any aquariums in the New York area had dolphins, so that she could volunteer and be around them.

About two years later, I was surprised to receive a letter from Marcia. Since I had been there when she agreed to explore dolphins, she wrote, I might like to know what happened.

She had bought a poster and put it over her computer. She had volunteered at the aquarium, spending many hours cutting up fish and swabbing floors. Eventually, she fell in love with the dolphin trainer. She was writing to tell me that she was about to be married, and that she and her soon-to-be husband were moving to Hawaii, to train dolphins together.

Shivers ran down my spine when I read that letter. Marcia's story is inspiring to people because it shows what magic can happen when they allow themselves to "follow their bliss," as Joseph Campbell suggested. A woman from Brooklyn, finding a life partner, and doing work she loves in a beautiful part of the world — it's like a fairy tale. However, it didn't require a fairy godmother, and it didn't mean taking huge, dangerous leaps of faith.

Marcia continued her work as a freelance writer while she volunteered. She stayed put while she explored this interest — she didn't abruptly pull up stakes and move to Florida to be "around dolphins." In short, she responsibly pursued her dreams and those dreams came true.

What if there was no Prince Charming? What if she never had the opportunity to move to Hawaii? She would still have been including dolphins in her life — and that willingness to be true to herself would have informed and enriched her life in other ways.

I've often used this story in workshops or in private sessions as a way of illustrating the concept of the power of listening to the inner voice and acting on it. Even the most diehard of my workshop attendees seem inspired by this story, and it offers them an example of how big and seemingly unattainable one's dreams can appear to be, yet still be within reach. Having heard this story, their own dreams don't seem quite as farfetched.

I was in touch with Marcia recently to interview her for this book. She still lives in Hawaii, and she and her husband now have a son. About this experience, she said:

> My internal message about dolphins was so clear, I just needed someone to reflect it back to me in that workshop so I could hear it.
>
> I am grateful that happened. As the years have gone by, I realize my internal voice has gotten really loud. And I can't ignore it, because if I don't listen, there are real consequences for me. I'm sure that's true for everybody, but if I don't listen to my inner voice, I find myself experiencing depression, misery, and resentment. What I've learned is that if you're not happy, you're not listening.

I love the simplicity and power of Marcia's statement — if you're not happy, you're not listening. Or, I might add, perhaps you're listening but not willing to hear.

Marcia's journey started in a workshop setting where we were all being encouraged to listen to that inner voice. Our leaders used techniques like meditation and guided visualization to assist us. I'm sure that made it easier. But you and I experience these messages every day if we are open to listening to them and acting on them.

It takes courage and a willingness to trust. It takes discernment to tease out what is wishful thinking and what is a true inner prompting. That requires time, patience and practice. These promptings are guides that help direct our steps toward an authentic expression of ourselves in our lives.

I have shared Marcia's story because it demonstrates so vividly the power of being true to yourself. If you feel that in some way you haven't been true to yourself, I hope Marcia's story will serve as an inspiration.

There are many reasons why people have trouble recognizing their inner voice, let alone being able to act on it. In this book, we will explore the barriers each of us faces in living a full color life. We'll also explore in depth the prerequisites to full color living, and we will discover valuable clues that will help you build a more fully expressive life.

Along the way, you will find ideas, tools and approaches designed to help you regain contact with your wise inner voice, and to help you take action toward your own full color life.

FULL COLOR REFLECTION:
THE INNER VOICE

Listening to the inner voice is a discipline that can be practiced. The first step is to find a place of peacefulness and ask that centered part of you for a response. Methods that quiet the mind, such as meditation or simply sitting in silence and focusing on an object or thought, can help the wise part within step forward.

Some people hear a response, others see one visually, still others get a gut feeling of what's right. Sometimes, when I am looking for guidance on a specific topic, I will sit in front of the computer, quietly center myself and try to disengage from any wishes or expectations I might have. Then I type in a question, place my hands on the keyboard, close my eyes, and type. What I find on the screen when I open my eyes is often a wise, calming response that takes a longer view than the current turmoil I may be experiencing.

Full color living is supported when we listen to the wise inner voice and act on its promptings. That requires being able to discriminate between all the competitive voices in our heads, and attend to the quiet, calm source of wisdom at the center of our being.

two

FINDING THE CENTER

It is important to tell at least from time to time the secret of who we truly and fully are — even if we tell it only to ourselves — because otherwise we run the risk of losing track of who we truly and fully are and little by little come to accept instead the highly edited version which we put forth in hope that the world will find it more acceptable than the real thing.

Frederick Buechner, *Listening to Your Life*

WHO AM I, *REALLY?*

Let's begin our exploration of full color living at the beginning. Our goal is to tell the secret of who we truly and fully are. For many people, that information is a secret even to themselves.

Before we get any further into the topic of who we are, I'd like to invite you into a brief exploration of who we aren't. We need to talk about identification. This is a huge issue that trips up many people on their way to full color living.

Being able to state with clarity who we are hinges on our ability to recognize and disentangle ourselves from our identifications. Our identifications are those external or internal aspects with which we align ourselves. An example of this is being identified with having a possession, like owning a sports car or Coach handbag, or drinking Starbucks coffee.

We can be identified with our appearance, with our political party, with our profession. These external identifications are a shorthand we use to communicate who we are. And while there is nothing wrong with owning a Corvette, there is a challenge if we are using the Corvette to define who we are: — that *successful, attractive, Corvette-driving person.*

Of course this is exactly what marketers target when they advertise their products. They sell the Corvette or the Starbucks coffee as the must-own item, so that by association we will be considered attractive and important by others. We reach automatically for these manufactured sources of identity, but of course they really do not define who we are.

We can also be identified with aspects of our identity, such as our race or ethnic heritage, or marital or financial status. Have you seen the movie, *My Big Fat Greek Wedding*? It was about a family's pride in their Greek heritage, and the heroine's struggle to affirm and accept the blessings and challenges of her heritage while also recognizing her individuality. Eventually she was able to recognize that while she is Greek, her ethnicity does not define her.

We can be identified with aspects of our past or upbringing. Are you a middle child? Did you come from a dysfunctional family? Were you successful as a student, or did you struggle? Were you part of the in crowd, or an outsider? What major events or relationships shaped your sense of who you are? Have these defined how you see yourself?

These identifications, while valid, can become all-encompassing, like the mother who, in her desire to be a great parent, loses track of other aspects of herself. Or the workaholic, whose identity is caught up in being successful and appreciated on the job, while forgetting about family, friends, health, and fun.

We've been talking about the external dimension of identification — relationships, our situation in life — what we see on the outside. So now, let's look inside.

Another kind of identification is with our personalities. Our personalities express themselves through an unlimited variety of individual traits. Yet, captivating as they may be, our personalities are also not who we are.

We are not our possessions. We are not our professions. We are not our associations, or our place in society. We are not even our personalities. Looks like we've eliminated a lot of possibilities.

At this point, if I were to ask you who you are, I wonder if you'd turn to the voice you hear in your head. That voice that directs you, criticizes you; repeats things over and over until it bores you, embarrasses you — you know the voice. We all hear it constantly. And here's the interesting thing: even this voice within is not who we are.

For many of us, that is an amazing concept. We can understand the idea of stripping away all that external information, but our inner voice is a constant companion. You might be thinking, "You're telling me that the interior voice is not me? At least, it is not all of me? Okay, then, who am I?"

And here's my answer. We are souls, first and foremost. At the center is the still, constant, reliable core within — our Self, our connection to spirit.

This is the home of the observer capacity, the fair witness that can see the whole personality system and everything else around it impartially, without becoming identified with any part of it. This is the part from which we can make choices and act in ways that are true to us.

We have all experienced this connection with the center. These are times when we feel clearly guided. We are not caught up in our typical fears and neuroses, we are not being driven by a need to please or achieve or impress. We feel open and at peace and grounded.

The spiritual teacher and author Eckhart Tolle writes powerfully about the process of becoming conscious and achieving this connection. He has an interesting take on our tendency to identify with that inner voice rather than with the center:

> Most people are so identified with the voice in the head — the incessant stream of involuntary and compulsive thinking and the emotions that accompany it — that we may describe them as being possessed by their mind. As long as you are completely unaware of this, you take this thinker to be who you are.[1]

"Possessed by their mind." What a great image. The antidote is to recognize this identification, and in fact all our identifications, and instead rest in the center.

This sense of I, of Beingness, is our connection with soul. It can be experienced in so many ways. I had one memorable experience of this as a 13 year old. I was alone, lying on my back on the end of a dock on Maine Island in British Columbia, looking up into the night sky. Being out in the country, there were no artificial lights to compete with the firmament, and the black, starlit sky felt close and vast at the same time.

I intuitively recognized a connection I have to something far greater than myself. I wasn't identified with being a teen-ager, a student, a girl, a daughter. My biography was irrelevant. I was larger, more spacious than all those labels. In these moments, our identifications are swept away and we recognize our true selves.

Often people experience these moments of connection in nature. Perhaps the change of pace or, literally, the slowing down that often happens when we take ourselves into nature, opens up an opportunity for just being.

FULL COLOR REFLECTION: BEING

Think about your own experience. When have you had moments of connection, when you felt your identifications fall away and you were simply at peace?

What conditions seem to have made it easier to step away from all the identifications and just be?

These experiences of the center are priceless examples we can use to recognize this place in the future. They also point you to activities or choices that will help you strengthen your connection to your center.

What would make it easier for you to have this sense of connection in the future?

Our discussion of identifications has been more than an academic exercise. We enjoy the identifications that make us distinctive — our possessions, our styles, our stories, our charming peculiarities. Yet, there is tremendous value in recognizing, "I am not all these externals. And I am not just that voice inside my head. I am pure consciousness and I have a direct connection to spirit and wisdom."

Why? It is from that centered, dis-identified place that we can hear guidance and skillfully respond. It is from that unencumbered place that we can make choices that help us build a full color life. The center helps us stay connected and whole and true to ourselves. That is why it is our beginning point.

Yet, we don't operate in daily life from the ether of beingness. The center needs the means to act in the world. To do that, we engage the personality.

Tom Yeomans, who directs the Concord Institute training program in which I spent two years learning about spiritual psychology, described this well:

> The soul and the personality are interdependent. The personality needs the guiding principle of the soul for its own development. The soul needs the integrity, beauty and development of the personality for its expression.[2]

The soul needs legs and the personality provides them. The center is the reliable core from which the soul directs, so that the personality can act.

three

THE INNER COMMITTEE

Each of us is a crowd.
Piero Ferrucci

One way of looking at our personalities is to recognize that none of us is a single person. In fact, most of us have within us many different focuses, styles, or qualities, which emerge depending on the situation. We might call these our Inner Committee.

The character George Costanza from the TV show, *Seinfeld*, gives us a colorful introduction to the inner committee. In one episode, he is upset because he is being forced into a situation where Relationship George and Independent George are in conflict. He is trying to keep them separate, but they still threaten to collide.

It could be fun to try to guess what other parts might reside within George — maybe Angry George, Neurotic George, or Manipulative George? I would throw in a few more positive examples, but the Seinfeld characters self admittedly didn't have a lot of redeeming characteristics. Most of us have both positive and negative aspects within.

We each have an entire cast of characters rolling around in our psyches. During my training in psychosynthesis[3], these characters were introduced to me as sub-personalities. Other approaches use different names but much the same concept. These are patterns of identity and behavior we unconsciously create as ways of coping with life.

At any moment in time, unless we are resting in our center, we are typically embodying one of these inner parts.

Some inner committee members are common to many people — archetypes such as 'the invisible child,' 'the loving mother,' and 'the martyr.' Others tend to be specific to individual experience; they can be very particular and intriguing. Once we identify them, it helps to choose a descriptive name that captures their energy and personality.

Some examples I've run across are 'the monk,' 'the bullshit artist,' and 'Petulant.' You may be able to identify a few of your own inner, more obvious committee members. Or, perhaps, you are more than familiar with someone else's. My friend Jeanne Liberkowski told me, "My mom has a strong Queen. Our problem is I don't have a strong Subject!"

By becoming aware of these aspects of our personality, we can recognize when they are dominant. Conversely, we can also work to bring out those parts of us that hold promise.

Sometimes an inner committee member has a tremendous gift to offer and it is important to find ways to give it more space. For example, a woman who for years has put others' needs ahead of her own might want to develop 'the Empress', a part of her that expects attention and respect. Or someone who for years has been accused of being overbearing might work to develop 'the sensitive listener.'

Keith Merron is a management consultant who is very aware of the importance of self-awareness both in his life and his work. Keith describes his experience with an overactive inner committee member:

A part of myself I'm getting to know more is 'the Driver.' It is so powerful that I sometimes believe its approach is *the right way of living*.

I believe this part of me evolved from my childhood. I grew up in an extremely high-achievement environment with two very successful parents who had expectations higher than the rooftops. So inside of me was this awareness that in order to be loved, I had to achieve extraordinary things. In order to achieve, I had to be driven.

I've been driving myself ever since. That Driver in me thinks this is the way. The good side is I do achieve — I have accomplished some significant things — built a successful business, authored books, etc. And, of course, there is nothing wrong with that. But it is a problem when it takes over. When I'm unconsciously in the grips of my Driver, I miss things that are valuable.

I can relate to Keith's story. I learned about one of my overactive inner committee members years ago, and she has a lot in common with Keith's Driver. I call her the Drill Sergeant. I have a detailed mental picture of her. She is short and square in shape. She has brown, badly permed hair. She wears a military style uniform, including sensible lace up shoes and support hose.

The Drill Sergeant doesn't think I am ever doing enough. When I am in her grip, I know that I am tremendously off center and not likely to come up with anything of value. She rushes me past all creative moments.

The good thing is that now I recognize her. When I see myself in the grip of this inner committee member, I need to stop, take a breath, figure out what she is afraid of or trying to accomplish, and redirect my attention. I need to consciously step out of the energy of this part of myself, and choose a different approach to the moment.

We often encounter an inner committee member when we are under stress. They are default positions we automatically embrace in order to get through a difficult time. As you read this, have any of your more familiar inner committee members come to mind?

We can also choose to identify and strengthen less-developed yet valuable parts of ourselves. For example, I also have a sub personality I have named 'Self-Expression'. I nurture this part of myself, wanting to bring her out more, by providing time and space for creative activities, and by surrounding myself with things that are colorful and inspiring. For example, the desk chair I use when I work is draped with a beautiful, jewel-toned scarf. That is a small reminder of this part within. It doesn't always require big things; often little moments of attention and acts of intention will help an emerging part of ourselves to blossom.

Besides the parts of ourselves that we recognize, or are working to strengthen, there are the parts we may wish to ignore or avoid. These parts aren't necessarily negative, they may simply feel uncomfortable. Yet they're part of us, and acknowledging them and bringing them to light is the healthiest thing we can do.

Keith describes his struggle with a less-than-comfortable part:

> For me, embracing the part of me that can feel joy or tenderness has been a challenge. It is far easier to embrace anger, or other more masculine parts of myself, than those more tender parts. But living in full color is embracing all of ourselves, including the parts we haven't owned.

Keith believes we all have some part that we haven't brought out because we're afraid, unwilling, or simply haven't figured out how. He told me, "For you, it could be the masculine force. And this book you're working on could be the vehicle to bring it forward in the world, to manifest it."

That was a very intuitive comment because I think he is right. I have shied away from the more direct, assertive, masculine part of me — and I acknowledge that it could offer much to me and to my work. I would be wise to spend some time giving this part more definition and expression.

In the exercise that follows, you'll have the opportunity to explore your own inner committee members. This is a good time to bring out your drawing materials — and enjoy!

FULL COLOR REFLECTION: YOUR INNER COMMITTEE

If you are curious about your own inner committee members, there are a variety of approaches you can take. You can simply name the ones you're familiar with, and try to be mindful about when you are unwillingly in the grip of one, or take action to strengthen another.

If you enjoy visualization, you might try an exercise taken from psychosynthesis. Get some drawing paper and colored pencils, and find a quiet spot. Close your eyes, center yourself, and imagine you are at an airport, waiting for an arriving plane. The first five characters off that plane will be your inner committee members.

Allow each of them to disembark, and as they slowly walk by, take a good look. You might see a young child, a clown, a polished professional, a derelict, a buoyant puppy, someone akin to my drill sergeant. . . the possibilities are endless. (I included a puppy in the list to make a point: because we're dealing with imagery, there is almost no end to the ways in which your imagination might translate the essence of a part of you. So if you see a cartoon character, or animal, or something inanimate, don't worry, just make note of it!)

> Once you've seen them, draw them as best you can. Try to capture the energy they present. Name them. This is a great start to becoming more aware of your personality system, and better able to recognize and disengage yourself when you are being run by an inner committee member, rather than being in charge and centered.

Our personalities are the instruments on which our soul plays. We've just looked at one fascinating aspect of the personality — our inner committee. Next, let's explore other ways in which your personality offers you clues to a full color life.

four

CONDITIONS FOR FULL COLOR LIVING

Our deepest calling is to grow into our authentic selfhood, whether or not it conforms to some image of who we ought to be. As we do so, we will not only find the joy that every human being seeks — we will also find our path of authentic service in the world.

Parker Palmer

SELF-ACCEPTANCE

We've talked about the value of listening to the inner, centered voice. We realize that doing so often involves letting go of expectations that have been internalized — from society, from our family, or from within ourselves. That inner, centered voice is the reliable source of guidance and direction, because it is connected to our higher wisdom.

We've also explored our inner committee members — those particular and sometimes less-than-helpful aspects of our distinctive personalities. Often, rather than listening to that clear guiding voice at our center, many of us find that these inner committee members are in charge and are making a lot of noise. And frequently, the loudest voice is that of the ubiquitous *Inner Critic*.

The inner critic is the foe of self-acceptance. It is a powerful inner committee member, sanctioned by society and likely nourished by the voices of those around us — parents, teachers, bosses, and others. Often we don't need anyone else to tell us where we fall short; we are fully prepared to identify our faults ourselves. And we do so, relentlessly.

Learning to be comfortable in our own skins is a lifelong task for most of us. Eighty-eight-year-old Carol Lehman Winfield says:

> It's only with age that I began to live uncritically. That to me is the difference between the wise old people and the heady young people. In general, old people stop being so critical, they just acknowledge and accept.
>
> And I think it's easier to do that when you're older. We're not going to get smarter; we may get forgetful, but we won't get dumber; and we're not going to get richer or poorer unless somebody hits the lottery — or something like that. We're not going to expand our friendships that much, so *where we are is where we're going to be*, and there is nothing we can do to change it except to acknowledge it with a positive view. And that's what I've come to do.

In his book, *Consulting Mastery*, Keith Merron (who was also interviewed for this book) speaks of the value of self-acceptance: "The more I am able to be gentle with myself, the less judgment I have about myself, the more capacity I have to learn, grow, and effectively be in the world."[4]

What an interesting concept, and how different from the standard approach to personal growth, which constantly emphasizes self-improvement. Having an attitude of self-acceptance not only feels better, but it can actually lead to being more effective. As we are able to accept and honor ourselves, it becomes easier to treat others with acceptance and compassion.

Psychiatrist Jack Weltner is a therapist and consultant, dividing his time between two community counseling centers and a private practice. With both a professional and personal interest, he has been delving into the world of psychology and emotions his entire career. He chronicles his journey on his website, http://www.safe-harbor.cc, where I found this inspiring message about self-acceptance:

> The freedom to be openly myself has been a huge relief. All the energy I used to put into keeping up some sort of appearance — of normality or of competence, or, worse, of being a hotshot — I can now put into living my real life.
>
> Also, I am freer to become who I really am instead of who I think I should be. I do think that one of our goals in being here in these lives is to become truly ourselves, as different and quirky as possible.

For many people, this concept of being able to live our real lives, without trying to hit some external or even internal standard, is life-changing. Often it comes as a result of a crisis, after which the person decides, 'Life is too short, I want to live my life the way I choose, and I am fully happy with that.'

But it doesn't require a crisis to make that decision. We can all accept ourselves as who we are and celebrate our different and quirky splendor. Maybe that takes courage. But as Jack says, with the willingness to be *who I really am* comes a huge relief.

It is liberating to let go of the pressure to try to be someone else! And it's equally healing to trust that *who we actually are* is absolutely fine and good.

Self-acceptance certainly doesn't come automatically to many of us. Fortunately, it can be learned, mastered, even celebrated. Carol Lehman Winfield teaches yoga to men and women in their 70s and 80s.

Carol explains that every yoga class ends with a celebration of self-acceptance, starting with a blessing:

> *I wish you to know joy, deep down, uninhibited joy.*
>
> *I wish you to have the courage to do and the courage to be what you want to do and want to be.*
>
> *I wish your spirits to find peace and your hearts to practice compassion.*

She explains what comes next:

> Then we open our eyes and we stand in a circle and raise our right hand and say, 'We!' and then we raise our left hand and say 'Are!' and then with both arms up we proclaim, '*Magnificent!*' WE ARE MAGNIFICENT!
>
> And it has an effect! I think it's so important to have this view. It's the total culmination of life — feeling that you are really magnificent and that your life is magnificent because *it is*! We are miracles. Even the lowliest of us. The fact of our existence is a miracle. The fact that we're able to survive is a miracle. It should be joyful.

I am not suggesting that goals are unnecessary or that self-improvement efforts are ill founded. We all want to learn, grow and improve. However, these efforts need to be rooted in a solid foundation of self-acceptance.

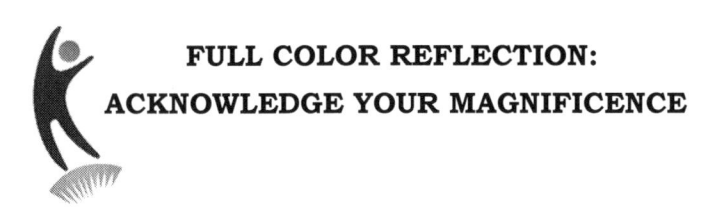

FULL COLOR REFLECTION: ACKNOWLEDGE YOUR MAGNIFICENCE

Why are we so willing to deny our own magnificence, thinking there is some target we haven't quite reached, some expected perfection we haven't attained?

What would it take for you to acknowledge that you are just fine — even magnificent — just the way you are?

How would self-acceptance affect the decisions you make every day?

What one thing could you do that would lead to greater self-acceptance?

AUTHENTICITY

To be nobody but yourself — in a world which is doing its best night and day to make you everybody else — means to fight the hardest battle which any human being can fight, and never stop fighting.

ee cummings

Authenticity is putting self-knowledge and self-acceptance into action. It means behaving in ways that are true to yourself. Often, it involves making a decision from your center, rather than from ego or some fixated part of yourself. Do I choose what I think is expected of me, or required of me; or do I choose what feels honestly right to me? And can I do this when it is inconvenient or difficult or even scary?

Not doing this causes stress, pain, even, ultimately, disease. Therapist Michael Brown takes up this topic:

> What causes the stress that brings my clients to seek therapy? My experience says it is the attempt to be what others say they must be, in order to be successful, important, to be respected.

That's a powerful message — the stress, which has caused enough pain to propel someone into therapy, is the result of denying our authentic selves.

Authenticity is played out in all areas of life. It can involve decisions such as choosing the job that feels inviting or exciting, rather than the one that makes the most sense logically. Or, paying attention to Thoreau's warning — beware of any enterprise that requires a new wardrobe — wearing the clothes that fit who we are and what we do. Or it can affect our choice of lifestyle and friends, or where we choose to live. By definition, authenticity requires inner honesty and, often, it compels external honesty: walking the talk.

Karen Van Dyke currently works in the banking industry, although she's not the stereotypical banking professional: for years she ran her own event marketing business, and she once spent a season playing a 'scaracter' at Universal Orlando's Halloween Horror Nights while substitute teaching during the day. Karen has made a lifelong practice of being honest with herself and others.

After years of self-employment, Karen is now daily addressing the challenge of living an authentic life while in a corporate setting. She has found one trait to be invaluable:

> I thank God for the things I brought into the corporate life to support me. I speak my truth, and I'm not afraid to do that. When I feel something is not right, I will speak up. I think silence is what kills people.

Megha/Nancy Buttenheim is a nationally recognized leader in the field of Kripalu yoga, movement and dance.

She is the director of Kripalu DansKinetics Teacher Training and Kripalu Yoga Teacher Training at Kripalu Center.

During our conversation, Megha talked about her commitment to speaking and living authentically:

> One of the most important aspects of yoga is the practice of Satya. Satya means "truth" in Sanskrit. I do my best to live authentically and always speak my truth, even when afraid of others' reactions. The Satya practice is a helpful riverbank for me. Nowadays I can easily see when I collapse into silence due to fear. When that happens, I do my best to return to my essential self and say what needs to be expressed.

Authenticity is informed by self-awareness. Jill Ramsier, Marketing Vice President for a high end restaurant chain, says that being true to herself became crucial to her happiness — but first she had to learn about herself.

Right out of college, Jill was married to "a great guy." "About three years into the marriage," she recalls, "I realized it didn't feel right. I love him, but I'm not *in love* with him. I began to wonder, what is this all about?"

After a period of exploration, Jill came to the conclusion that she was gay. However, she was afraid that besides its obvious impact on her marriage, acknowledging the fact would disappoint her parents and be an obstacle in her career. She couldn't see a way to act on this new self-awareness without causing tremendous damage. So she stayed in the marriage, while feeling increasingly alone and unhappy.

Then a loss caused her to rethink the situation. Her best friend from graduate school passed away from cancer at age 27. Deeply affected, Jill soon after made the decision that life was too short to remain in a marriage that was not right.

Jill and her husband divorced, and she went through a tough time, feeling guilty for acting on her feelings. But being authentic put her on a path to happiness: "Today I am in a wonderful relationship of five years and the happiest I could ever be." And it turned out, her ex-husband ultimately recognized that the marriage hadn't been ideal, and is now happily remarried.

We may struggle with acknowledging and accepting the truth of who we are, but truth is mandatory for an authentic life.

The experience of failure often begins with a lack of authenticity. The relationship between failure and authenticity was a central theme in a book to which I contributed: *Song of the Phoenix, The Hidden Rewards of Failure*. I interviewed people in a variety of circumstances who had experienced what they considered a significant failure.

Through these interviews, I realized that in cases where the person had chosen the word 'failure' to describe his or her experience, some degree of that person's true identity had been lost or substituted or denied. What they considered failure was, in fact, a collapse of inauthenticity.[5]

Interviewing these people was a very rich experience for me. In effect, this project was a practicum about the extremities of life. People eagerly shared stories of alcoholism, broken marriages, extreme poverty, business failures, career disasters, nervous breakdowns, school failures and other experiences. Having weathered these, my subjects had come out the other end somewhat battered but vibrant. They had used their experiences to grow stronger.

We all have life experiences that could be labeled failures. But they are also profound redirections that help us find our true paths. They give us hard-earned wisdom about ourselves and what matters to us. They reroute us toward greater authenticity.

Marcia Mager, who we met earlier, sees authenticity as the key to happiness:

> My entire life I have been committed to living authentically. When I'm not, I'm profoundly miserable. It goes in stages and levels and spirals — there'll be a period of living from my heart and passion, then I drift away, then I notice how unhappy I am, and that will propel me to look deeper. I ask, 'Where is my passion, where is my heart?' Then I'll find it again.
>
> It's a process and it keeps changing. *I cannot live inauthentically.* And I guess that's a tremendous blessing, because there seem to be people in the world who can live inauthentic lives and go to their deaths that way. If I find myself living inauthentically, it's like having a noose around my neck and I wake up and say 'Oh shit. I can't do this anymore.'

In his book, *The Highest Goal*, creativity expert Michael Ray notes that authenticity is transformative:

> Once you quit striving so hard to be someone or something that you aren't, you can find your own brand of creativity and success, and transform what you already have within into something positive. You can be ordinary. Instead of fighting who and what you are, you simply get clear about it. The goal is to take the energy that exists and find harmony with it.[6]

Psychiatrist Jack Weltner was talking about this earlier — the relief of being able to just be yourself, of being ordinary. I wonder if you find this idea as astounding as I do — the idea that it is okay, even ideal, to quit striving and simply be. To follow what comes naturally, without effort.

So many of us work so hard to become someone, not recognizing that we already are someone. Instead of engaging in the struggle, what happens if we allow ourselves to follow the flow of our natural inclinations? What happens if we allow ourselves to be ordinary, in our individually magnificent ways?

That expansive, creative, unburdening place is the land of authenticity.

FULL COLOR REFLECTION: AUTHENTICITY

What aspects of yourself do you tend to avoid, ignore, or reject?

What barriers do you experience — internal or external — to living more authentically?

What one change or decision would help you live more authentically today?

five

FULL COLOR EMOTIONS

ABOUT FAMILY SYSTEMS,
or, "The Marvel of the Mobile"

I will never forget a presentation I attended during a period of focused exploration in my early adulthood. It was one of those 'aha' moments for me.

Dr. John Messerschmitt came one evening from the local community counseling center to speak to our adult education group. His topic was how our experiences in our families of origin (the families we grew up in) have the potential to impact us throughout our lives. He brought a mobile, the kind you might hang over an infant's bed, to illustrate a family system; with each brightly colored shape representing a different family member.

To show the impact of dysfunction in the system, Dr. Messerschmitt pulled down one of the shapes and held it in place. Immediately, all the other shapes bounced into a new formation. They adjusted to bring equilibrium to the system.

He was demonstrating a common problem: when one family member is dealing with some form of dysfunction, such as mental illness or an addiction, everybody else has to adjust to help bring the family into some kind of balance. Typically, according to family systems theory, we will adjust by taking on a role, our task in the family. The spouse or partner is usually the enabler. The children unconsciously choose among several common archetypes: the hero, the mascot, the lost child, and the scapegoat.

Taking on these roles is a natural and reflexive adaptation to the situation. But, Dr. Messerschmitt asked, what happens when we leave our family of origin and enter the world as an individual? We have become very good at the role we played in our families; in fact it was automatic. We may not be aware of playing this role, and may not realize that it is no longer needed.

This was an 'aha' for me because I had grown up in a loving but dysfunctional family system, and had automatically taken on the role of hero — the good child who gets the grades in school and is no trouble at home. I could also recognize my younger brother and sister among the typical roles.

The other 'aha' idea that Dr. Messerschmitt presented that night was the concept of family myths. He said that families create myths to help them tell their story in a way that is more comfortable than the reality they are living. I still remember how that concept rocked me. It was a brand-new idea, and it was true. My fantastic, crazy, dysfunctional family had a big myth: *Everything is wonderful.* It didn't matter if the bills weren't getting paid or we were constantly on the move, everything was wonderful.

Having grown up believing in a myth, it has taken me years to learn how to look beyond the words to the reality. Over time, I understood better how this myth impacted my own thinking. As I became more aware, I also felt tremendous compassion for my parents, especially my father, who so wanted that myth to be reality. I want to believe in the myth, but as an adult it is important that I see what is true.

These two pieces of information — about dysfunctional family systems and family myths — opened my eyes to the fact that I had been formed by powerful forces. If I wanted to live a conscious life, I would need to learn about how my upbringing had formed me. I would need to step out of the role I took on as a child, and let go of the family myth that was so attractive but ultimately dishonest.

FULL COLOR REFLECTION: FAMILY SYSTEMS AND MYTHS

Before we go further, I invite you to think about your family of origin. Was there an 'identified patient' — someone who was acting out with alcohol, drugs, violence, or other behaviors? Were you able to be yourself, just a child, or were you conscripted into some other role? If so, how have you come to terms with this role, and have you learned to set it aside when it is not helpful?

Then, was there a family myth to which you all adhered? Can you put it into words? Some examples of family myths might be, 'The parents are always right,' 'Evidence to the contrary, Uncle Marty is a sane and happy man and we treat him just like everyone else,' 'Everyone in our family loves each other,' 'Every family member is destined for success!' You might tease it out of your subconscious by saying the phrase out loud, 'In *this* family, we always/we never/...' Once you have a sense of your family myth, think about how this unquestioned belief may have impacted you as a child, and may still be influencing your thinking today.

Next, let's recognize the positive outcomes of your upbringing. I encourage you to consider the gifts that

> came from your family of origin. What rich traditions were handed down to you? What positive beliefs and behaviors have you taken with you into your adult life and your own relationships? What blessings from your past bring you gratitude today?

OUR EMOTIONAL GUIDANCE SYSTEM

When you try to force your feelings to submit to your mind, it's like throwing away the map to a happy life.
Barbara Sher

Our emotions are trusty guides. While often we would rather ignore them, or try to change them, the wiser route is to listen to them.

Let's explore the rich source of wisdom that resides in our emotions — and how being attuned to our emotions can guide us toward full color living.

Early in my working life, I had an interim job as executive secretary to the newly hired president of a technology company. He had been brought in to help a high tech startup make the transition to world-class competitor.

The president was a hard-hitting man who had grown up in a challenging environment and put himself through school working in a steel mill. He described his work as a young man — spending his days alternately freezing or in blistering heat. He had no soft edges, although I suspected that beneath a very gruff exterior hid a sensitive soul.

This man was demanding and rough with his subordinates, and consequently had a hard time earning their genuine support. Beneath the surface I sensed a roiling hot river of anger. At times during staff meetings I would be taken aback at his aggression. Something in his inner life was impacting his ability to lead successfully.

One day I got a call: he wouldn't be in for a few days. He had been hospitalized with damage to the esophagus. He literally had been spitting blood.

'Spitting blood' was an apt metaphor for his behavior. I would like to think that in subsequent years this highly qualified executive came to terms with his emotional life, so that it would support, not interfere with, the rest of his life. But I don't know if he did.

Our emotions cannot be dismissed, buried, ignored or denied for very long before they demand to be acknowledged. That is a good thing. It may take some time before they become so obvious as to defy our effort to ignore them. Eventually they are bound to break through.

Once we become aware of negative emotions, the first step is to do some learning and healing. Let's look at an example of another man who was also dealing with anger, but, unlike the executive, he paid attention.

Ric Reid is a highly regarded Canadian stage and film actor. He identifies himself as having been an 'angry young man' and realized over time that his unexamined emotions had the potential to destroy him. Ric recalls:

> I was an emotional kid. I had strong feelings. I empathized with others. Seeing a friend miss a home run at little league could make me cry, but my father explained to me that this is not behavior we show in public. In my world, as a jock, you were only allowed anger. Anything else was unacceptable.

Being a good kid, Ric followed directions. He shut himself down emotionally, negating all his feelings except anger. While he easily landed the 'angry young man' roles, over time this strategy took its toll:

> The only saving grace that got me through it was the belief that life is not supposed to be this miserable. You put anger out in the universe and it comes back at you. I knew I wasn't meant to be this angry and doing so

much damage to myself and those I cared about.

Ric's profession ultimately saved him:

> Acting requires that you explore psychology — you have to get as close as you can to walking a mile in someone else's shoes. I started to be able to see things from different points of view.
>
> As I grew in my craft, I became more emotionally vulnerable. I think the reason I am drawn to be in this creative performance world is my need to understand emotions — my own, and others.' In order to be a better person, to be a better lover, father, husband, and son, I needed to have a better grasp.

With his awareness deepening through his work as an actor, Ric sought counseling to help him understand and work with his own emotions. Eventually, he was able to share what he had learned with his father:

> My father was one of those stalwart 'boys don't cry' men. I think he was also deeply emotional, but he never allowed himself to be. When he turned 60, I said to him, "I am going to tell you what I think of you and I will continue to do this for the rest of our lives together because it needs to be said."
>
> What I said to him was, "I love you." It was a shock to him! Here was his adult son, saying to him, "I'm going to be emotional, and it's going to be okay, we're both going to survive."

Ric concludes, half-seriously, that in his opinion every male member of our society probably needs some counseling:

> Chances are, if you're a man, you have been shut down emotionally, either through your football coaches, your parents, uncles, or whatever. There was a code of behavior that denied emotions, and what you haven't learned to do is accept them. Men don't

understand. Emotions are not feminine. They're human.

Ric's story illustrates how a family myth, or shared cultural belief, impacts the experience of a child. 'Boys don't cry' was a rule that Ric couldn't challenge as a young boy. He adapted in order to get along, but at a price. As an adult, Ric recognized that to be whole, he needed access to all his emotions.

Another man I interviewed recognized the role of emotions in his own life, and now it is his job to help others do the same. Peter Lund is a hospital chaplain working with sick and terminally ill children and their families. Peter regularly sees what happens when people try to avoid their emotions, especially in the highly charged situations faced by his families. He explains:

> I work with families who are in crisis. Often they try to soldier through the crisis without recognizing and accepting their emotions in the midst of it. The model in our culture is you go to work and leave your inner life behind. Just disengage from it.
>
> With fathers, when they're trying to parent kids through a crisis, they have this sense of drawing a line between their own tumultuous emotions inside and their expectations of how they should behave. And it usually is the father who will have the most trouble with this.
>
> What I do with parents in these situations is to ask, "What is going on inside of you? Let's look at this expectation: *being strong is not showing any emotion*. What is *that* about?! What does that teach your children? What does that do to you?"

Peter notes that in these high stress conditions, without the ability to acknowledge and accept how family members are feeling, emotions end up 'coming out sideways' and causing a lot of anxiety and unintended crisis. On the other hand, addressing the emotions can be incredibly freeing and can help draw families together during this most difficult time. For Peter, full color living requires recognizing our emotions, acknowledging their value, and accepting them regardless of the circumstance.

Whatever the challenge — a lack of awareness that we have these emotions, not understanding where they come from and why they're here, or unwillingness or inability to acknowledge and express them — the result is suffering. There's an opportunity here. Pain can be a powerful motivator for change.

Our automatic response to a problem or to an emotion we are trying to avoid is to lock it up in the unconscious. Ric tried to bury every emotion except anger; out of sight, out of mind.

It takes a lot of energy to keep unresolved emotional trauma out of sight. That energy could be much better used for growth and creativity. In bringing emotions out into the light and resolving the underlying problem, there's an explosion of liberated energy. Not only is this healing, but in addressing and healing buried or rejected emotions, we open the door to new experience.

So there's the payoff. Whether we choose to acknowledge and work with challenging emotions, or they just break through, we are presented with an opportunity. We can gain awareness and understanding. We can make choices and changes. We can liberate all that stuck energy and make room for new possibilities.

And we may need help along the way. At various times in life, each of us will be faced with a crisis, problem or emotion we can't deal with alone. Life is cyclical — there will be periods of calm, and then all of a sudden something big is happening — an opportunity for learning and growth, although possibly wrapped in an unappealing package. At times like these, a therapist or wise friend can be an invaluable conversation partner, to help us gain awareness of the situation and navigate towards wholeness.

In times of relative calm, we have the opportunity to increase our awareness of our emotions very simply on a daily basis. Marcia Mager is a published author whose story about dolphins you read earlier. She offers simple guidance:

> Pay attention to how you feel. When you wake up in the morning, or you're traveling to your job or you're at work, check in with yourself: how do you feel? If you can't access your feelings, what are you thinking about, where are your thoughts going? Look around. Are you happy?
>
> If the answer is no, that's the first place you have to be. So acknowledge your unhappiness, dissatisfaction, or lack of nourishment. That can be a process in itself.
>
> Then, begin exploring what would bring you more joy. Of course this involves listening to the deep place in yourself that was able to even hear this question — because if you can hear the question, 'What's missing?' that's the same place that will say, "Go take a painting class or start gardening or travel."

If you want to live a life of full color, start by listening to your emotions. They will guide you. But you need to become friends with them first.

HOW TO BE TRUE

six

DISCIPLINES OF FULL COLOR LIVING

The quality of life is in proportion, always, to the capacity for delight. The capacity for delight is the gift of paying attention.
Julia Cameron

The #1 point made by the people I interviewed for this book was this: pay attention. When I asked them, "What do you think is most needed in order to live a full color life?" they consistently said, "Pay attention. Be present. Live in present time."

Frankly, this is not the response I expected. As someone with a lifelong interest in translating gifts and interests into vocation, very much on the 'doing' end of the continuum, I was stopped in my tracks as time and time again, the interviewees pointed to dimensions of being.

Yet, it should come as no surprise that we need to be told to stop and pay attention when we live in a world that seems designed to distract us from ourselves. We are always on the move. To get it all done, we multitask (although scientists tell us we are deluding ourselves because our brains can only focus on one thing at a time). What we are really doing is interrupting ourselves over and over again.

I have been in plenty of meetings where people paid more attention to their blackberries than the conversation.

Every third driver is also having a cell phone conversation. Recently, my husband came out of a public restroom and told me that a fellow in one of the stalls was on the phone — and had initiated the call *after* he went in! In my opinion, that's taking multi-tasking to unnecessary lengths.

As we send our attention out in all directions, we lose track of ourselves. Compounding the problem is a common societal expectation that to be successful we must consistently juggle a variety of tasks while operating at top speed: 'Look at Jones, he is so important he has to do three things at once to get his job done!' Feeding this frenzy is the ego, which desperately wants to be seen as successful. It would be funny if it weren't so sad.

Operating at top speed without truly paying attention can have serious consequences. I'm sure many decisions which are later regretted were made under these conditions.

Plus, there is the toll on physical well-being. It has been estimated that 75-90% of all visits to primary care physicians are for stress related problems. Think about that! What an unnecessary physical, emotional, and financial cost.

Our calendars are overbooked. We believe we will have a better chance of checking everything off the list if we move quickly and try to do everything at once.

Instead, let's put on the brakes for a moment. Let's slow down. In their book, *Creativity in Business*, Michael Ray and Rochelle Myers explain why this is a good strategy:

> If you pay attention at every moment, you form a new relationship to time. Your own absorption slows you down internally. That slowing down feeds your sense of deep appreciation and at the same time produces more energy. In some magical way, by slowing down you become more efficient, productive, and energetic; focusing without distraction directly on the task in front of you. Not only do you become immersed in that moment, you *become* that moment.[7]

Slowing down enables us to pay attention. Slowing down also helps us recognize what is important to us. It is a discipline that fine arts professor Diane Tarter recommends to students in her two-dimensional design class:

> I tell my students to notice the small moments. They inform what's important to you. It may not be a visual thing, it may be something about emotional response to the irony, the humor, whatever it is, that trips something you can use later.
>
> These moments are telling you what's important to you — the kind of things you notice, the kind of moment you appreciate, catching a snippet of a conversation as you walk by, the quality of light as you're driving home, being connected to the world. It's not an endless stream of experiences, it usually happens in smaller, intense moments.
>
> If you know where those moments tend to be, pay attention to them. Those are the kinds of things to notice in your life, probably the things that are telling you who you are and what you're good at.

We don't need to be design students to heed Diane's advice. Every day, we race past moments, impressions and messages that are so rich and valuable. In our hurry to accomplish, we miss the true content of our lives.

Pausing on purpose is an excellent antidote to busyness, and provides a window of opportunity to become more conscious of the details of life. As we bring awareness to the present moment, we become more conscious of the marvelous specificity of our experience. We bring awareness to our senses, whose contributions are often overlooked.

Through attention I am able to fully enjoy the taste of each bite of my meal. I feel and smell the lovely breeze rustling the papers on my desk. I become aware of the presence of my dog, as I hear his regular breaths at my feet.

Paying attention is a discipline that becomes easier as it becomes more habitual. Slowing down helps tremendously, so the first step often is to catch yourself as you rush through your day, and bring yourself to a centered place of focused attention.

FULL COLOR REFLECTION: PAY ATTENTION

What would happen if instead of speeding up and doing several things at once, you were to slow down and allow yourself to give your full attention to just one thing, until you are ready to move on to the next just one thing? How would that change your experience?

Stop for a moment, and pay full attention to the information coming to you through your senses. What do you see as you look around you right now? What do you hear? What smells are near you? What do you feel — the solidness of your chair, the heat of the sun, the breeze from your overhead fan?

Were you aware of all these senses before you stopped and consciously paid attention? What difference might it make to do this more often?

MEDITATION

The gift of learning to meditate is the greatest gift you can give yourself in this life.
Sogyal Rinpoche

We have been talking about slowing down and paying attention to the present moment. As we've noted, that is not always an easy thing to do.

Many people who are searching for an increased ability to be present in their lives turn to meditation. If you are not already familiar with meditation, I hope this will inspire you to draw on a technique that is tremendously supportive to full color living.

Meditation is a discipline that encourages us to stop, breathe, center ourselves, and let go of that chattering mind, finding a wonderful resource of stillness within. It takes us out of our concerns about the past or the future, and keeps us squarely in the present. It offers a way to dis-identify with the ego, and reconnect with our true selves, that unchanging center of pure awareness.

As a simple, no cost antidote to the busyness of modern living, meditation creates a quiet oasis for clarity and renewal. A daily practice of even a few minutes can help us find that spacious place of inner connection.

Jon Kabat-Zinn, founder and director of the Stress Reduction Clinic at the University of Massachusetts Medical Center, has worked extensively with mindfulness training. His book, *Wherever You Go, There You Are,* provides a gentle introduction to the practice and value of meditation. In the book he notes:

> People think of meditation as some kind of special activity, but this is not exactly correct. Meditation is simplicity itself. As a joke, we sometimes say: 'Don't just do something, sit there.' But meditation is not just about sitting, either. It is about stopping and being present, that is all.[8]

Chiropractor Dean Nelson points to meditation as central to his ability to live a full color life:

> You need the bravery to open your heart and make profound friends with yourself — become present to yourself. Without that, you're pretty much a cork in the water. Are

you willing to sit down and pull the plug on all the entertainment? The classic, most proven way of doing that is meditation.

Because it quiets the mind and helps us become centered, meditation is also one of the best routes to developing a connection with our intuition. The discipline of meditation strengthens our ability to reliably access our sixth sense, adding a rich source of knowing and clarity.

Classes in meditation are widely available. Often, yoga classes incorporate meditation practices as well, which not only gives you the value of stilling the mind, but also reconnecting with the breath and the body. And while meditation is a personal experience, there is a wonderful power and community created when a group of people meditate together.

PRESENCE

Awareness is the power that is concealed within the present moment. That is why we may also call it Presence. The ultimate purpose of human existence, which is to say, your purpose, is to bring that power into this world.

Eckhart Tolle

Presence is resting at the center of your being. It feels like being solid, calm, unattached, and open. It means having no agenda. The ego is not in charge.

I experience being present and the presence of my classmates at the end of yoga class, when we all emerge from a guided meditation absolutely grounded in our bodies and spirits. The demands of our world have yet to press themselves on us; we are serene and content and centered. We try to sustain this state of mind and heart as we leave the room and return to our lives.

Let me give you an example of the opposite. Have you ever been in a group that is taking turns to speak — maybe they're introducing themselves? Have you noticed that while one person is speaking, you (and the others) are thinking about what you will say about yourself — so that by the time it is your turn, you have figured that out, but haven't quite taken in the other introductions?

This is an example of not being present — the mind is elsewhere while the body is here. How often each day are we divided in this way? I firmly believe this is our normal state much of the time.

Instead, the practice of presence suggests that you can simply fully listen to each person, then when your time comes, your words will also come. You can be present to them, and present to yourself.

I was part of a training program that had a conscious discipline of practicing presence at times like these. We found that by truly listening with full attention, you are giving something of real value to the other person, and to yourself. What needs to be said gets said, and everyone is heard. Plus, the entire experience is less stressful and much more enjoyable.

Being in the company of someone who is truly present is an affirming experience. What has been your experience with this?

By definition, a therapist should be fully present to his or her client. When a parent is fully present, the child feels welcomed and heard. When friends are present, we sense their full interest and support.

Presence is a stance we take on life. When we are present, we fully embody the moment. We commit ourselves to paying attention and sharing ourselves in the moment. We honor others and ourselves through this gift of attention.

It begins with developing this ability within ourselves — of not being distracted, not having a burning cause to pursue, but simply sharing ourselves in the moment. This requires letting go of expectations and assumptions and opening ourselves to the joy and possibility of each moment.

Poet and author Roger Housden describes the result:

> ...as one falls present to oneself, it is more natural to be present with others. At home in your own skin, it is more likely you will feel at home, not only with your intimate others, but also in the world.[9]

LIVING IN PRESENT TIME

The only thing we really have is nowness, is now.
Sogyal Rinpoche

This is a tough topic for me. As I am working on this book, I suspect I am being mocked by the universe because I am having such trouble living in present time. I try to make a practice of recognizing the present moment and living in present time. Usually I'm better at it — not so much right now.

Now that our children are launched into three different cities and their adult lives, my husband and I have decided to move from our present home in Orlando to Sarasota, Florida, two hours away. We are both looking forward to living in a smaller city, near the ocean, with a wide variety of arts and plenty of opportunity for tennis and other activities. However, first we need to sell our current home, and the real estate market has a lousy hangover following a wild ride up over the last few years.

I know that when the time is right, our home will sell and we will be free to move. I believe that God is directing our way. It is entirely possible that the home we are meant to have in Sarasota hasn't even found its way to the market yet. And yet, with all this 'wisdom,' I am having a real challenge with living in present time, here in Orlando, in our unsold home. So I write this section for myself as much as for the reader!

The present time is where our life experience takes place. I know this is true. We can't live in the past. We can't live in the future. Only the present moment is available to us. This moment. This moment. This moment.

And I realize there is a danger in allowing our spirits to drift back into the past or forward into the future. Intuitive healer and author Carolyn Myss suggests that for every time zone that we are in, other than the present, we drain our life energy. We need to keep our spirit in present time.[10]

And keeping in present time doesn't require that life is smooth and easy. I could certainly learn from the experience of non-profit administrator Barb Wood as she navigated the next steps of her life following a job loss. It was not a huge blow; she had been ambivalent about the job for some time, and in fact had already begun laying the groundwork for her next career. At the same time, this job loss didn't take place on her timetable, and it abruptly launched her into a series of decisions about where to live and what to do next.

Yet, having spent the past few years investing heavily in her own personal growth, Barb was prepared to respond to this period of 'not knowing' with grace:

> I feel really blessed with all the options out there, very spacious, excited about hanging out in the ambiguity of not knowing what is next, until the right thing comes along. And I trust I'll know that right thing — it seems there are infinite possibilities. I'm glad I've done as much work as I have, it is definitely showing up now with feeling calm through this.

Home, work, and community were all up for grabs, yet Barb was able to rest in the present moment as she responded to inner promptings and made plans for the future.

My favorite folksinger, James Taylor, sings with simple accuracy about living in the present:

> "The secret of life is enjoying the passing of time.

Any fool can do it.

There is nothing to it."

Enjoying the passing of time. Doesn't that make you think of people sitting on the front porch on a warm summer evening, chatting with neighbors, sipping a cool iced tea? Can't we have experiences like that today? Of course we can.

Slow down.

Become centered.

Pay attention.

Be present to yourself and others.

Live in the present moment.

These are the daily disciplines of full color living.

seven

FULL COLOR PERSPECTIVE

Start every day off with a smile and get it over with.
W.C. Fields

IT'S ALL ABOUT ATTITUDE

Viktor Frankl, who wrote *Man's Search for Meaning* in response to years spent in a concentration camp during the Holocaust, said that the last of the human freedoms is "to choose one's attitude in any given set of circumstances, to choose one's own way."

I can't imagine anyone more qualified to make this assertion: regardless of the situation, the one thing we can always control is our response to it.

Certainly every one of us, at some point in life, deals with major life changing experiences like the death of a loved one, a serious illness, financial crisis, or loss of a relationship. It can be hard to hold your head above water, let alone maintain any kind of perspective. These times feel far more black than full color.

Although Frankl reminds us it is possible to choose our attitude even under great duress, my view is that in these cases, most of us first need to find support and take time to heal.

But let's focus for now on times that are less grave and more commonplace. Think about your average days, full of typical challenges, stresses, inconveniences, disappointments. How do you choose to respond?

Some people, and you may know one or two, live life surrounded by a fog of pain and unhappiness. Perhaps they are very identified with their wounds — an unloving mother, a deceitful friend, an unfaithful spouse.

Perhaps they see themselves as ill treated, unlucky, unable to claim their place in the world. When I was in theatre school as a young adult, a commonly held belief was that it was impossible to be truly creative without being miserable, and so gloominess became a mark of talent.

"It's very much easier to be tragic than it is to be comic," noted novelist Robertson Davies. "I have known people who embrace the tragic view of life, and it is a cop-out. They simply feel rotten about everything, and that is terribly easy."

To add insult to injury, by dwelling on the negative, we only attract more of the same. It becomes a way of life, an endless feedback loop of negative experience reinforcing negative experience.

If you see any of this behavior in yourself, the first step is to recognize this worldview, and decide to respond differently. Chiropractor Dean Nelson recommends this starting point:

> "The key thing is that you fully, fully, *fully* get out of victim mentality about your life. Whatever the circumstances you're in, it's still yours to do something about."

I once heard of a wonderful exercise that can help you experience for yourself the power of a change in attitude. Tell some aspect of your life story to a friend three times. First, tell it as if you were a victim. Then, tell it as if you were a hero. Then, tell it as if you were a person who learns and grows from experience. See how these different perspectives make you feel.

I'll give you an example from my own experience. I grew up in a family that was overwhelmed by alcoholism. Because the money went to liquor, we couldn't afford other things like rent, and we moved constantly. To give you a sense of how this played out, by the time I finished second grade, I had attended five different schools.

So, with my victim hat on: "I didn't get the stable childhood I deserved. I don't have friends from when I was young because we moved so much. People shouldn't expect much of me considering what I went through. *I never had a bike!*"

Next, with my superhero hat on: "It is amazing that I have come as far as I have considering my upbringing! I must be incredibly smart or talented or otherwise highly gifted!"

And putting on the hat of the person who learns and grows from life experience: "It is true that my upbringing was challenging, but one thing we did have in the midst of it was love. And out of all that moving, I developed the skill of entering new situations, meeting new people, and not being afraid. That has been a real benefit in my career."

Regardless of my life experience, I can choose not to be a victim. I can choose not to cast myself as a larger-than-life superhero, inflating myself into some unrealistic, unrecognizable shape. Instead, I can choose to recognize what happened, address any lingering pain or unconscious behavior through counseling, and identify and acknowledge the strengths and positive aspects that emerged in me through this experience.

FULL COLOR PERSPECTIVE

FULL COLOR REFLECTION: CHOOSE YOUR ATTITUDE

> Do you have a big story that could benefit by this exercise? I gave you an example from my experience — think of one of yours. Then write down your story three times.
>
> -First, tell it as if you were a victim.
> -Then, tell it as if you were a hero.
> -Finally, tell it as if you were a person who learns and grows from his or her experience.
>
> As you look over this story, told in three different ways, see how these different perspectives make you feel.
>
> Which perspective would you like to use in the future?

Attitude is something we can choose, even when we can't control the circumstances. Karen Van Dyke is a manager in a corporate environment that she finds very challenging. She influences change where she can, but also recognizes that as long as she chooses to remain, she needs to be able to operate effectively within the existing culture. She explains her approach:

> I make the choice to be positive because the people I work with deserve that. Otherwise you bring each other down, and what the hell is the point? Smile and see how you feel, then frown and see how you feel — which way do you want to feel? I make the choice to be positive because it's healthier for me and for the people I work with.

So, step one — check your attitude. Are you in victim mode, or otherwise making excuses for not fully inhabiting your life? Are you in denial, pretending that everything is fine while clearly there are problems? Or are you able to stand firmly in reality, with the recognition that you can tell your story and make daily decisions from a place of empowerment, choice, and positive expectation?

APPRECIATION

When my kids were six and nine years old, we traveled to New Orleans to visit their uncle, who was in law school. It happened that their grandparents were also in town for a conference, and they offered to take us to breakfast at one of New Orleans' finest hotel restaurants, a place we never would have considered on our budget.

The dining room was elegantly appointed. The table was dressed with linens. The servers wore white gloves and poured hot chocolate and coffee out of shiny sterling pots. This would clearly be a grand occasion.

We studied the menu and discovered several tempting choices, but we all went with the house special, Eggs Benedict. My mother-in-law, however, couldn't join in as she was on a diet. She ordered two soft-boiled eggs and dry toast.

The service was attentive, our cups were refilled, and soon our meals arrived. Everything looked fabulous. We dove in. My mother-in-law sliced into one of her eggs with a knife and immediately proclaimed loudly and accusingly, "This is *not* my idea of a three-minute egg!"

The deferential waiter responded immediately, whisking the offending plate away to fetch new, more precisely timed eggs. Our entire table was silent, mortified by the over-the top-outburst in this gracious environment. Under his breath, my son summarized what had just happened with one word: "Pow!" And then we all laughed.

This story is a lighthearted example of what happens when we deny ourselves the experience of life in all its glory. My mother-in-law must have been feeling resentful, seeing Eggs Benedict all around as she contemplated her two eggs and dry toast. While moderation is sometimes necessary, in general, life is a grand buffet and nothing less. And when we take part, we fully appreciate what is offered.

Appreciation is a powerful emotion. We talked earlier about the experience of being in victim mode, and drawing negative energy as a result. Appreciation does the opposite. If like attracts like, then appreciating what we love attracts more of the same.

Many spiritual leaders assert that before we do anything, we need to begin with appreciation. In her article, *The Magic of Appreciation*, author Lynn Grabhorn said:

> The vibration of appreciation is the most profoundly important frequency we can hold, for it is the closest thing to cosmic love that exists. When we're appreciating, we're in perfect vibrational harmony with our Source energy, or God energy — call it what you will.

You've met Carol Lehman Winfield — she's a yoga teacher in her late 80s. Carol doesn't need anyone to tell her about appreciation — she's all over it — a fabulous example of enjoying all life has to offer:

> You're talking to a hedonist at heart, you're talking to a totally whacked-out woman here! I love food, I love sex, I love sunshine, I love my grandchildren, my great grandchildren. I vibrate to almost everything. Life has so much to offer and I want to try it all!

And although I have been reminiscing about silver serving dishes and white linen tablecloths, when I asked people about what was important to them in their lives, they spoke instead of simple things. It's interesting that while automatically we want to do and have more, happiness depends on much less.   Lanie Delphin is a matchmaker in Massachusetts. While her business often makes her day busier than she might wish, she describes herself as a domestic person who prefers a balanced life. She told me:

> I don't need fancy trips or a fancy lifestyle. I derive great pleasure from the details. I am very enthusiastic and passionate about the little things like healthy, delicious food, movies, books, good TV, plays, shopping, learning, taking walks, and especially sitting with friends around the kitchen table.

In contrast, I asked international Food & Beverage executive Dieter Hannig about his version of a full color life. In his work, Dieter has traveled extensively, lived in a number of countries, and dined frequently at the finest restaurants.

Not surprisingly, for a professional chef, the good life includes food, but not necessarily at a gourmet restaurant — Dieter also appreciates the peacefulness of home:

> I always come back to food when we talk about a good life. . . I come home from work and my wife cooks, or we cook together. There is no stereo blasting, no television. I always have two bouquets of fresh flowers; that's my visual stimulation. And there's nothing better than smelling real, fresh food. There's time to talk.

> So you create your own stage setting, and just focus and breathe. It's paying attention in the moment and appreciating small things, like going out to the garden and cutting fresh mint to make tea.

Appreciating each moment is key to full color living. Spurring the desire to seize the day is the recognition that our days are numbered. The present is all we have. People who are living in full color find ways to bring joy to each day.

It may be appreciating a tiny moment, or creating a rich and exciting one. It may be gathering friends around a table, cutting fresh mint from the garden, or just stopping in the midst of a busy day to take a few deep breaths of fresh air.

Megha, whom you met earlier, has created a daily practice of appreciation:

> Gratitude is deeply important to me. I have written in gratitude journals as a spiritual practice for decades. First thing every morning I write down a list of the things I'm grateful for. Each day it's something different. If it's a gorgeous morning, I'll write "clear blue sky," or something about my family. I might write in celebration of finishing a project. If going through a difficult time, I might write that I'm grateful to be just sitting with the issue until it resolves itself.
>
> I often recommend gratitude journals to my students who suffer from depression. It's a lovely panacea. I think four of the most important words in the English language are "I'm sorry" and "thank you." Being grateful makes life worth living.

Hundreds, maybe thousands, of these moments invite themselves into each of your days. They stand at the doorway, hoping to be noticed. See them. Welcome them. Appreciate them. Celebrate them. These small moments are in fact the stuff of life.

EXPLORATION

*You know you're dying when you're playing not to lose.
You're living when you play to grow.*
Richard Whitely

Life moves in two basic directions — expansion and contraction. Full color living generally requires that we be open to new things, expanding in one or many areas of life — knowledge, horizons, skills, passions, perspectives, social circles, experiences. It pits the desire to expand against the fear we have when faced with something new. People who are living in full color find meaningful ways to explore while acknowledging and moving through their fear.

My son has always been an adventurous eater. Whenever we went out to eat, Cooper made it a practice to find something new. When he was about 10, Buffalo wings became popular, and he decided to try them. His impression? "They're good, but they taste just like chicken!" In the years since, Cooper has sampled chicken feet, squid, octopus, alligator, snails. . . "I'm always up for new things," he says.

Greg Mort suggests that as an artist, and in life, an attitude of exploration is foundational:

> I draw inspiration from lots of things. If you think of where the ideas for a painting might generate, I guess you might go to a lot of museums. Of course that's not it at all. That's some of it. That gives you an idea for what is possible in the manipulation of materials, but it doesn't generate the stuff of ideas. That comes from everywhere.

And what happens once the inspiration hits? Greg responds:

> If I get an idea for something that grabs my interest, however bizarre it is, I'll do it. People talk about the blank white canvas, that's just too scary for them. They think, 'I've bought this thing; what if I wreck it?' You can't have that attitude about painting, and certainly not about life. You have to be willing to take risks.

Living with a spirit of exploration can lead down many roads. They don't all necessarily arrive at the expected destination, and that is okay. Parker Palmer writes:

> There is as much guidance from God in what does not happen and cannot happen in my life as there is in what can and does happen. Maybe more. . . Every time a door closes behind us, the rest of the world opens up in front of us. All we need to do is stop pounding

on the door that is closed, turn around, and see the largeness of life that now lies open to our soul.[11]

Jack Weltner, the psychiatrist you met earlier, speaks to this from his experience:

> So many of us get caught in the everydayness of our life as if that's what dominates us. Every once in a while I think *"What's next?"* because everything has become too easy. You don't know what's going to work. The only way to find out if it is really interesting is to go in and see if it resonates with something inside.
>
> The other factor is if the gods want it to happen. Some of the doors I open would be perfectly lovely, but when I go down that path, it doesn't lead anywhere. Or sometimes you do something for a while and then it dries up. It's great when you're fully involved in it. When it gets to be routine, when there's no fire in it, it's probably a good time to move on.

Jack speaks with understanding and compassion about the quixotic nature of life. Sometimes we set a goal, and we find ourselves right where we expected. Sometimes we head off in a new direction, and find that what once looked promising reveals itself as a dead end. Sometimes we simply realize that we've done something too long and it's time for a change. Being willing to explore and try new things is the challenge — and it helps to be open-minded about the result.

It also helps to be flexible about how we approach new experiences. Back in my theatre days, I was part of a small company that was auditioning actors for a production of Molière's *The Misanthrope*. We saw their prepared audition pieces, then had the actors pair up and play a scene from the script.

I will never forget one young man. After we had invited him and an actress to read a scene, he grabbed her arm and, while speaking his lines, proceeded to drag her around the stage.

We stopped the scene. "What are you doing?" I asked. "Oh," he said. "I've done this." We finally figured out what was going on. He was auditioning for a role he had done in another production, using the blocking from that performance, ignoring the fact that he was putting his acting partner in an impossible situation. He was trying to reproduce another experience instead of responding to the situation in the moment. He didn't get the job.

Often, taking the leap marks the beginning of a whole new phase in life. Diane Tarter remembers one memorable decision:

> I've always known that if I needed to do something it would hit me and I would try to do it. My desire to do it would overcome the fear. For example, right after college I decided to go to England for further training in theatre. That was big for me.
>
> The most scary and independent moment I've had was walking out across the tarmac to the plane. I looked back at the waiting area windows where I knew my family was standing. But the windows were mirrored on the outside. I waved at the place I knew they were, but I couldn't see them. I saw the reflection of myself waving, but I couldn't see them waving back. Then I stepped on the plane and off I went. It was a metaphorical moment, the beginning of the next stage in my life.

Carol Lehman Winfield says that exploration has been a natural response to her desire to experience life fully:

> Something about me is greedy to experience and see and absorb as much as I can. During the Second World War, my husband was a flight surgeon. So I decided to learn how to fly. I earned a pilot's license, and I did it because I

wanted to be closer to him and find out what it was like to be in an airplane.

Dieter Hannig and his family consciously built exploration into their lives:

> My wife, son and I made a focused effort at least once a year to get into an environment we didn't know. I think it's important to stretch outside your comfort zone. So, for example, if we're arriving in a big city we don't know, we'll ride the subway instead of getting a taxi to the hotel.
>
> We always got a kick of out of this. Although sometimes it can get scary — we took a couple of trips where we didn't speak the language or we got lost, and all of a sudden you're huddled up in a hotel room wondering if you did the right thing! But we feel it's worth it because it opens up your horizons, and stimulates your thinking about all these aspects of life — culture, people, food, art, and religion.

Psychiatrist Jack Weltner maintains that the spirit of exploration goes hand in hand with a willingness to look foolish. He decided to take up the tuba, and he finds joy in playing it, even though he admits rather gleefully that he plays badly.

Jack's stance on this?

> To hell with dignity! I think dignity is the enemy of freedom. Saving face limits our capacity to have fun, to be real, and to be at home in our flawed selves. Playing tuba badly has been good for me. . . Not having to look good gives me the freedom to try new things.[12]

Sometimes a spirit of exploration can lead to a transformed life. Lanie Delphin had just such an experience:

> I moved away from where I had been living for 20 years, was remarried to a wonderful man,

changed my name, bought a new house and changed careers.

If you had told me ten years ago that I would be living in a new community with a different life altogether, I'm not sure I could have taken it all in!

Exploration looks different for each of us. For some, it can involve trying a new food or a new hobby. For others, it's leaving an established home for an unknown place. It can include learning new skills, meeting new people, seeing new lands. It is expansive, growth promoting, and an important aspect of full color living.

FULL COLOR REFLECTION: EXPLORATION

What is your next opportunity for exploration?

- ☐ Learning a new skill?
- ☐ Trying out a hobby?
- ☐ Taking a trip somewhere new?
- ☐ Joining an interest group?
- ☐ Becoming active in a community group?

Choose one or two specific activities that would bring more fun and interest to your life, and look for a way to include them, starting now.

eight

CLUES TO FULL COLOR LIVING

We don't always know what makes us happy. We know, instead, what we think should. We are baffled and confused when our attempts at happiness fail... We are mute when it comes to naming accurately our own preferences, delights, gifts, talents. The voice of our original self is often muffled, overwhelmed, even strangled, by the voices of other people's expectations. The tongue of the original self is the language of the heart.

Julia Cameron

Why is it that the clear information we have even from childhood about who we really are is so easily obscured from us as we get older? Do we automatically decide that having reached adulthood, we need to play by someone else's rules and abandon our true selves?

As a parent, it is abundantly clear to me that we each come into this world with distinct personalities, passions and gifts. My son Cooper has been a sports enthusiast since he was a young child. He didn't get that from his parents. When he was 10, he explained to me the NCAA chart he'd drawn up to track the basketball season. He followed the season with devoted interest, game by game. Now, as a young adult, he will travel great distances by plane, train or automobile to take in his favorite team's games.

His sister Kate, who as I write this is graduating from college with a BFA in drama, was drawn to the stage at an early age. Her first role was "Mrs. Beaver" in a school production of *The Lion, The Witch and The Wardrobe* at age five. They are who they are.

When I look back at my own childhood, I also displayed a theatrical bent at an early age, and teachers counseled my mother to harness my energy. "Keep Jennifer busy, or she'll end up on the stage!" they warned. (I guess she didn't keep me busy enough, because I did end up on the stage.)

But isn't it harder to see these things in ourselves than in others — and more challenging yet to act on what we know?

Many of us discover that the inner voice that successfully and naturally guided us into engrossing and pleasurable activities when we were young becomes overruled by reality as we get older. Choosing between college or career options, we are warned, 'Jobs in that field are too hard to find,' 'That doesn't pay well,' 'People in our family don't do work like that.' 'That's not a real career, get serious!' And then what happens?

The author Parker Palmer speaks to this:

> We arrive in this world with birthright gifts — then we spend the first half of our lives abandoning them or letting others disabuse us of them. As young people, we are surrounded by expectations that may have little to do with who we really are, expectations held by people who are not trying to discern our selfhood but to fit us into slots. . . We are disabused of original giftedness in the first half of our lives. Then — if we are awake, aware, and able to admit our loss — we spend the second half trying to recover and reclaim the gift we once possessed.[13]

The great psychologist Jung said that the psychosis of our century is to separate ourselves from our true selves. This separation leads to tremendous pain, dysfunction, even illness. In the course of interviewing a wide variety of people on the topic of full color living, I heard a distinct, unanimous message of how to live a satisfying, fully self-expressive life: Be True To Yourself.

Be true to yourself. Sounds simple. It certainly isn't original. Hundreds of years ago, Shakespeare famously had Polonius advise, "To thine own self be true."

But how do we do that?

We have explored some of the prerequisites to full color living, such as paying attention, appreciation, living in present time, and adopting a spirit of exploration. Now let's explore several sources of guidance that provide specific clues about your particular full color life. In this chapter, we will delve into your unique passions, gifts, strengths, and vocation.

PASSION

If you follow your bliss, you put yourself on a kind of track that has been there all the while, waiting for you, and the life that you ought to be living is the one you are living.

Joseph Campbell

What are you passionate about? What do you love? What do you do just for fun, because of the intrinsic reward, or because the experience is so enjoyable? Passion is a spark God implanted that provides wisdom and direction. Full color living involves following our bliss and making room for the expression of our passions, our loves, every day.

Our passions tend to be consistent. When I was exploring the idea of writing this book, I looked through my library to see what books I had been collecting over the years. There are a few on crafts, a few on gardening, some on travel, but by far the biggest collections are on topics of personal growth, spirituality, and vocation.

Your books or magazines may be on entirely different topics. The point is, passion points us to our gifts, and our gifts guide us to our vocation.

Some people's passions seem to overflow and are obvious from an early age. Did you have any friends in grade school who displayed a single pointed fascination and attraction for art, math, gym, writing, or some other subject? I suspect a lot of us envy these people, especially if we are having difficulty owning and acting on our own passions.

The passion of the great television personality and chef Julia Child was unmistakable. She inspired the culinary world and millions of fans who watched her cook on television. Her belief was, "It's fun to get together and have something that is good to eat at least once a day. That's what human life is all about — enjoying things."

Julia has a kindred spirit in Jill Ramsier, the restaurant marketing executive we met earlier. For Jill, a passion for cooking and sharing food with others came from childhood. She explains:

> I love food. I love wine. When I'm not at work, I'm cooking. I cook all day long. I love having people over. I love hosting.
>
> Every room in my house has cookbooks or cooking magazines in it. Or wine books. I'll sit down and start reading the Oxford wine dictionary and my partner will say, you're reading the *dictionary*?
>
> I learned to cook and got the passion from my grandparents. One grandmother was Hungarian, the other Polish, and they would cook these amazing meals. And I would cook with them.
>
> It was the social center of our life. We were all so busy with school and sports, but when we cooked together or all sat down to the table, it was a time to connect. It was a time to put

everything else aside and focus on what you're doing.

And I've carried that through. I love to cook because it takes me out of any stresses of life; it allows me to focus on pleasing others. It's really calming to me; it's an amazing feeling. It's an outlet for enjoyment and self-expression, but fortunately it's also part of my work. So, for example, I have earned the designation of Level I Sommelier (wine expert) and I'm working on level two, and I get paid for it!

Another example of someone who paid attention to his passion is Will Shortz, the New York Times crossword puzzle editor. I first heard his piece on NPR's *Weekend Edition* — he offers a puzzle each week for the listening audience. Later, watching the documentary film about Will and the American Crossword Puzzle Tournament, *Wordplay*, I learned that he persuaded Indiana University to let him design a degree program in <u>enigmatology</u>, the study of puzzles.

What do you suppose his parents thought? "How can someone make a living making up puzzles? Is there really a call for that?" Well as it turns out, there is, and Will Shortz gives us a great example of following one's bliss.

FULL COLOR REFLECTION: YOUR PASSIONS

Make a list. What fills your spirit? What is rejuvenating, engrossing, inspiring to you? Our passions are so specific to us and such reliable guides. Do you love music? Conversation? Kayaking in the wilderness? Hosting people? Repairing things? Spending time with animals? Researching your family lineage? Making order out of chaos? Being with children? Gardening? Exploring the world?

Some of these passions will likely be about activities you like to do just for fun, things that enrich your life. Others will be guides to your gifts and your vocation.

FLOW

Before I had kids, I had a vegetable garden. Our landlord, who lived next door, plowed a large oval field in the back yard every spring. I was new to gardening and in my enthusiasm (and lack of knowledge) planted enough seeds and young plants to feed a fraternity.

Having a big backyard garden was not uncommon; we were in the country and all my friends had gardens. Late in the season, at the height of production, it became almost an affront to bring a gift of fresh vegetables when going to a friend's for dinner; especially zucchini, which was prolific. At this point, no one could get rid of the zucchini they had in their own gardens. By August, you'd see massive, overblown zucchinis used to hold down tarps; they were as valuable as rocks.

My experience of gardening, once I got the hang of it, was transforming. I would arrive home after a day's work, throw on an old pair of jeans and a flannel shirt, and spend a good hour digging in the dirt. I discovered that all the concerns of the day floated away. I couldn't focus on them, even if I wanted to.

My attention was entirely caught up with pulling this weed, digging this hole, tidying this plant, watering this row. Slowly and steadily, I made progress on my garden. Time flew by. Eventually the light would fade, I'd realize I was hungry, and I'd go in.

This was an experience of flow, of losing myself in an activity and, in the process, losing track of time. It was engrossing and satisfying, and while I had an overall goal in mind, I was able to focus and be present during the experience.

Psychology professor and researcher Mihaly Csikszentmihali has spent much of his career exploring what creates this experience of focused engagement in everyday life. He started by studying artists, because they typically describe being satisfyingly lost in their work.

But Csikszentmihali discovered that this experience translated to many other aspects of life, including hobbies, work, even to everyday tasks like driving a car. He also identified several typical factors of a flow experience.

True flow activities typically have clear goals, provide unambiguous feedback, and engage us in using our skills to overcome a challenge or reach a desired outcome. Attention is ordered and invested and the person becomes completely focused. This naturally occurs when engaged in a favorite hobby, like gardening, but it can also take place at work.

An important element of flow is that it requires not only our attention, but also our effort. Yo-Yo Ma certainly is a naturally talented musician, and Michael Jordan a natural athlete, but both of them reached the pinnacles of their fields because of their commitment to refining those talents into full mastery. Achieving the full promise of flow requires applying ourselves to the effort.

The experience of flow is of being truly engaged in an activity. It involves something we are good at, our effort and focused attention. Experiences of flow are brightly lit signposts on the road to full color living. Think *neon*.

What happens if we put passion and flow together? An activity for which I have a passion and in which I also experience flow is what I'm doing now — writing on a topic I care about. In this case, the experience of flow tells me that this is not just something of general interest to me; it may be something that merits my time and effort.

FULL COLOR REFLECTION: EXPERIENCING FLOW

What activity allows you to lose track of time? What captures your attention and holds it? What do you enjoy enough to be willing to invest the effort in mastering it?

Have you found ways to include these activities in your life?

GIFTS

Now there are a variety of gifts, but the same Spirit; and there are varieties of services, but the same Lord; and there are varieties of activities, but it is the same God who activates all of them in everyone. To each is given the manifestation of the Spirit for the common good. To one is given through the Spirit the utterance of wisdom, and to another the utterance of knowledge according to the same Spirit, to another faith by the same Spirit, to another gifts of healing by the one Spirit, to another the working of miracles, to another prophesy, to another the discernment of spirits, to another various kinds of tongues, to another the interpretation of tongues. All these are activated by one and the same spirit, who allots to each one individually just as the Spirit chooses.

I Corinthians 12: 4-11

My first introduction to the concept of giftedness was a course on *"the theory and practice of the ministry of the laity"* at Andover-Newton Theological School outside of

Boston. It focused on the idea that lay people play a vital role in ministry, both within the church and in the world.

Being offered at a seminary, the course drew heavily from scripture. We explored the idea that we all have gifts, and they are unique to us. So, for example, while one of my friends is gifted at leadership, and another at being an administrator, I can claim gifts in communication. And it is okay, in fact part of the design, that we are not all good at the same thing. (What a relief that is!)

Our gifts point the way. We are drawn to use them. We are in fact required to use them if we want to live in full color. And before we go any further, I should note that another word used interchangeably with gifts is 'talents.'

It may be easier to recognize the gifts of a child, friend or co-worker than to name your own. Here are a few examples from my circle: My brother Stuart loves to work with his hands — he has tinkered with cars since he was a teenager rebuilding an MGB sports car. Now he owns a home renovation company. My sister Stella is a multi-talented singer and visual artist, who recently held an event in which she sang the songs that inspired each of her paintings before the audience snapped them all up.

And a few friends: Betsy has the gift of listening to someone describe a complicated problem, then simplifying it until the answer becomes clear. Jeannie has a gift of inspiring enthusiasm and excitement about a project. Marci is a natural leader, able to win support and commitment from her team even in challenging conditions. Luis has the ability to reach out and connect with people, putting them at ease. These are just a few examples of gifts I see around me. I'm sure you have equally rich examples from your community of family, co-workers and friends.

One of the most exuberantly gifted people I know is artist Greg Mort. From a young age, it was clear that he could draw, and as a young man he decided to see if he could make a go of it as a career.

Greg's paintings are displayed in major museums and collections both in the United States and abroad. He speaks with real modesty about his talent because, as he describes it, his ability truly comes from within — he doesn't make it happen; it happens to him.

During our phone interview, I asked him how he was able to be so prolific in creating his art. Greg explained:

> Right now we're having this interview, and as we talk, I'm working on a painting. How can I do that? It comes from a weird place that has nothing to do with any other place. So when I'm working on a painting, probably what I'm thinking about the least is the painting. It flows naturally, I don't worry about it, I'm just painting away. . .
>
> It was difficult at first to accept the fact that I was going to do this for my livelihood. I told people it was like getting paid for sleeping. It just comes out! I don't have to think, 'I'd better get to work.' I've never said that. It's something I'm instantly compelled to do.
>
> Often great bodies of time will go by and I have no awareness of it. I guess you could say it's a zen-like thing, because it's coming from this other part of you; it's almost like auto pilot.
>
> Here's an analogy — you can be out walking around having a conversation, but your heart is still pumping; you don't have to think about it; the body does it automatically. That's kind of how this is.

At the end of the interview he joked, "I would say I'll get back to painting now that we've finished talking, but I never stopped."

Greg has the advantage of a gift that is so clear and powerful that he would probably have trouble avoiding it. It has the internal subtlety of a Tom and Jerry cartoon where someone gets clobbered — in this case, with the incessant desire to pick up a paintbrush. Greg responds almost in auto pilot, with joy, and the result is inspiring.

It is easier to recognize the concept of giftedness in the arts. But we all have gifts — either evident from birth, or uncovered during a lifetime.

Many of us identify our gifts as we move through our lives and careers. Peter Lund is a hospital chaplain working with sick children and their families. Although it is emotionally challenging, it is also incredibly powerful and meaningful work, and in the midst of serious illness and even death, he explains, "You're part of some pretty wonderful and beautiful moments. You witness incredible love, and forgiveness, huge good and beauty in the midst of the pain and suffering."

Peter has discovered that beyond the knowledge and expertise he brings to his work with these families, one of his gifts is the ability to be calm while working in such a highly charged situation:

> One dad said to me, 'I've met other chaplains, but what I like about you is you seem to be able to talk to me without going, 'Oh, my gosh, how do you *live* with that?!' Instead, if I can calmly have a conversation with this parent, I can give something to that person. And I feel good knowing I was able to help him.

Arts educator Diane Tarter's career has evolved until she is now in a job that allows her to use both her technical skills and her gift of bringing people together:

> I have discovered that I really like talking to people who come to me for advice. I've had some of those flow moments when I was listening to someone and talking something through with them that they were trying to sort out.
>
> Interestingly, when the job of division chair came up, I didn't see myself doing it. But my colleagues seemed to think I was the right person for the job, so I said okay. And I've

> realized the fit: while half of my time is spent teaching, the other half is focused on administrative work, and that's when I can use what I know about situations at the university. I like thinking with others to help bring people together and make it work the best way possible.

Career counselor Barbara Sher was one of the first to write about the relationship between giftedness and career. I turned to her books as valuable resources as I developed my career in vocational counseling — and for my own personal exploration. Her first book, *Wishcraft: How to Get What You Really Want*, was one of the first I discovered on the topic of identifying passions and gifts and achieving goals.

Sher's message is uncompromising — she believes that we are *required* to identify and fulfill our gifts:

> Something inside you is calling to you and *you have to listen.* When you love to do something, that means you have a gift for it. And when you're gifted at something, *you have to do it.*[14]

Some gifts came as part of the package when we were born. Some emerged in response to challenges during our lives — the concept of wounded healer points to the gifts bestowed on people who have earned them through tough times. Some gifts are called out because of a need, like Peter's ability to be calm and centered with his families. Some gifts are quiet and behind the scenes, some wild and noisy. The main thing is that they are ours, and they are meant to be used.

STRENGTHS

> *The knowledge of what God made us good at is precisely what drains out of us as we supposedly grow up. It's not that every adult has forgotten it, just most of us. It's easy to spot the ones who have not forgotten what God made them good at. They are the happy ones. . . Some extraordinary*

> *adults remember what all ordinary children know: the key to life is to love what God made you good at and to do what you love.*
> Rabbi Marc Gellman[15]

Passion fuels us.

Our gifts guide us.

And our strengths enable us to reach our goals.

Until now, our exploration has focused on understanding ourselves in order to live more authentic and joyful lives. We have looked at our passions, at the activities in which we experience flow, and at our gifts.

As we journey further into the topics of strengths and vocation, we are contemplating our activity in the world, such as work or volunteering.

Former Gallup researcher Marcus Buckingham has been studying strengths for much of his career. Here are some characteristics he has discovered that can help you identify a strength[16]:

- ☐ You love to do it.
- ☐ You're good at it.
- ☐ You are drawn to it.
- ☐ You keep naturally developing your ability.
- ☐ You are fully engaged when doing it.
- ☐ After you've done it, you feel fulfilled and authentic.

A strength isn't something you love, but do badly — that might be better defined as a hobby. It's also not something you do well but dislike — that's a 'burnout skill.' A strength lives at that powerful intersection of great passion and high ability. And as Rabbi Gellman puts it, the key to life is to love what God made you good at and to do what you love.

The Gallup organization has conducted comprehensive studies for over thirty years on how to maximize potential in the workplace. They've learned that:

1. Each person's talents are enduring and unique
2. Each person's greatest room for growth is in the areas of his or her greatest strength.[17]

Their research says that it is far more productive to focus on and further develop what we do well than trying to fix what we don't. Organizations should build their human resources strategy on this insight, but typically, they don't!

In *Now, Discover Your Strengths*, the Gallup researchers report that they asked 1.7 million employees in 101 companies from 63 countries the following question: "At work, do you have the opportunity to do what you do best every day?" Only 20% said "Yes."[18]

Rather shocking, isn't it? That suggests massive amounts of lost potential, and likely also indicates a less than joyful workforce: if you're not doing what you do best every day, what *are* you doing?

Obviously, there is tremendous opportunity to improve organizational performance simply by identifying people's strengths and then ensuring that their work gives them an opportunity to use them. It requires letting go of the widely held belief that everyone has to be willing and able to do everything, and allowing people to focus where they can add most value.

If strengths are such important guideposts to a successful and satisfying career, it is imperative that we identify them and find ways to use them. Even outside of the work world, knowing our strengths will lead us to rewarding activities in which we can make a contribution.

Some people have a solid familiarity with their strengths. Others are a bit more vague on the topic. If you could use help shedding light on your own strengths, I recommend this simple exercise.[19]

FULL COLOR REFLECTION: YOUR STRENGTHS

Think back on your life, and make a list of accomplishments you're proud of. Review the highlight experiences in childhood, early adulthood, all the way to this moment. Your accomplishments don't need to be huge, wildly impressive, or work-related. All that is needed is that *you consider them to be highlights in your life.* Try to list at least 20.

Some examples to get you thinking:
- Throwing a successful party for your parents' anniversary
- Mediating a conflict between two co-workers
- Designing and sewing your first quilt
- Winning a debate match
- Researching and publishing your family history
- Repairing a car/dishwasher/watch/computer. . .
- Creating a dynamic, effective web site
- Coaching the team to a little league victory
- Raising a child to have compassion and self-confidence
- Performing in a band at the high school dance

You may also have work-related examples, such as:
- Hitting a challenging sales target in a down market
- Researching and solving a complex accounting error
- Designing and implementing a successful training program
- Achieving the highest customer service scores for your district

Once you've listed at least 20 accomplishments, go through the list and pick the five that mean the most to you. Then write a short story about each of these five accomplishments. Include what you did, how you did it, who you did it with/for, how it felt, using as much detail as possible.

Next, study these accomplishments and tease out the strengths that comprise them. Look over each of your stories. What abilities are demonstrated in them?

Look for phrases such as:
-Solving complex technical problems
-Mediating disputes to uncover shared agreement
-Inspiring new behaviors in others
-Challenging myself physically
-Leading under adversity
-Giving individualized care and compassion
-Creating beautiful and functional environments

These are just a few of the unlimited possibilities. . .

Having explored in depth your five favorite accomplishments, now draft a summary statement that defines one or two of your key overall strengths. In other words, what strengths are most evident in the accomplishments you chose?

Then, compare what you've written against the elements that comprise a strength. Does it fit?

-You love to do it.
-You're good at it.
-You are drawn to it.
-You keep naturally developing your ability.
-You are fully engaged when doing it.
-After you've done it, you feel fulfilled and authentic.

Now you at least have a solid first draft of those activities that inhabit the intersection of *what you love* and *what you're good at*. Knowing our strengths — and better yet, using them — is an essential component of full color living.

VOCATION

Becoming faithful to our gifts and inclinations, hearing the call or press within to be whole, we find vocation — that line of activity we intentionally use to grow as a person.[20]

Marsha Sinetar

Let me make one thing clear. No one I interviewed for this book started with the assertion that finding the right work was the answer to living a full color life. As this trend became clear, I must confess I was surprised. With a background in vocational counseling, I have always paid great attention to how people can find work that fulfills their needs, engages their passion and uses their gifts. I expected to hear more about the centrality of satisfying work, but I didn't.

This is not to say that vocation is unimportant; just not primary. What we've talked about so far — paying attention, living in the moment, the power of appreciation, understanding and accepting ourselves, being open to experience — these are the foundational things.

However, with these in place, and having identified and welcomed our individual passions, gifts, and strengths, identifying and pursuing vocation remains the next step in self-actualization.

What is vocation? It is the calling we experience to express our gifts in the world. It is where the rubber hits the road. Here is how author Frederick Buechner defines it:

> Vocation. It comes from the Latin word *vocare*, to call, and means the work a man is called to by God.
>
> There are all kinds of different voices calling you to all different kinds of work, and the problem is to find out which is the voice of God rather than of Society, say, or the Superego, or Self-Interest.

By and large a good rule for finding out is this. The kind of work God usually calls you to is the kind of work (a) that you most need to do and (b) that the world most needs to have done. If you really get a kick out of your work, you've presumably met requirement (a), but if your work is writing TV deodorant commercials, the chances are you've missed requirement (b). On the other hand, if your work is being a doctor in a leper colony, you have probably met requirement (b), but if most of the time you're bored and depressed by it, the chances are you have not only bypassed (a), but probably aren't helping your patients much either.

Neither the hair shirt nor the soft berth will do. The place God calls you to is the place where your deep gladness and the world's deep hunger meet.[21]

Where your deep gladness and the world's deep hunger meet. So it involves more than just doing something fun like beachcombing, but it doesn't require abilities we possess but don't enjoy, like filing.

And it is important to acknowledge that our vocation can change with time and experience, just as we do. I have known too many people who allowed their résumés to dictate their future career direction. They became trapped by their skills, knowledge and accomplishments when they'd prefer to head in a different direction altogether.

True vocation is at the intersection of what we love and do well, and what is needed — it allows us to use our passions and gifts, and in so doing make a contribution which is uniquely our own.

"Lovely," you say, "but how do I do that?" Discovering vocation can be something of a treasure hunt. We look for fragments of information in our biography and personal experience. These clues include interests, strengths, passions, hopes, expectations, relationships, successes, values, and much more.

So, for example, 'what I love to do with my spare time,' 'moments when I have had a flow experience,' 'activities that give me energy,' 'environments I find interesting'—all of these can steer us in the direction of vocation.

I had a conversation with a recent college graduate who was working in an hourly job while she tried to figure out her career direction. Alicia was confused about how to begin. It can be scary, especially at the beginning of a career when it seems that every decision is setting the stage for our entire life!

Here's what I said to Alicia:

> Imagine yourself standing in the center of a big circle. You could potentially go in any direction from here. But you already have plenty of information to help narrow your focus. You know what you like and don't like. You know the topics and environments that interest you. You know the kinds of activities you enjoy. You know what you passionately care about and what you're good at.
>
> So instead of having 360 degrees of possibilities, even at this point I bet you could narrow it down to maybe a 30° swath that is worth exploring. Turn away from all the other options, and start moving in that direction. Stay true to what you know about yourself and keep exploring. You probably won't find the 'perfect job' immediately, but you will find something that is much closer to what you will enjoy as a career direction. And with each step, you will get closer to your vocation.

Yet even if we have perfect clarity about what we most want to do, we have resistance to pursuing our vocations. There are almost limitless internal messages we can use to stop ourselves from moving toward our vocations. See if any of these voices of resistance sound familiar:

☐ We think we should do something we 'ought' to do, rather than what we want to do.

- ☐ We don't believe we can pull it off.
- ☐ We don't think we have the right to do something we love. 'That's for other people,' we say; we need to stay chained to misery.
- ☐ We are unwilling to turn away from years invested in a particular field, with all the knowledge and income potential it represents.

It can take a lot to overcome this resistance and many never do. Author Gregg Levoy puts it this way: "Most people don't follow their dreams until the fear of doing so is finally exceeded by the pain of not doing so, although it's appalling how high a threshold people have for this quality of pain."[22]

Being self-aware is helpful here. Are you feeling content with where you are, or stuck? Do you find your work stressful or rewarding? Are your strengths being used, or does your work require abilities that don't come easily to you? When Monday comes, are you raring to go, or trying to hide under the covers? Are you feeling energized and healthy, or do you drag yourself through the day, and find yourself getting sick more than you used to?

Matchmaker Lanie Delphin has found a vocation that fits with her passions and strengths:

> I run a business where the skills required are my strongest: caring about people's wellbeing, being nonjudgmental, being able to listen and remember everyone's stories, being intuitive, being lighthearted, and being able to teach and coach people. Bringing folks together who would never have had a chance to meet is certainly profound and taps into my somewhat romantic nature. My stepdaughter says I have an uncanny ability to say anything to anyone, even if it is negative, and not sound mean. I think my heart coming through my voice in all my interactions is my greatest asset.

The perfect job isn't a requirement for full color living. That's lucky, because most of us at some point will find ourselves in a job that is less than a great match. And there are times when we need to make a tradeoff. For example, a young parent might take a less than ideal job because it offers flexible hours while the children are small. Or we may be in a difficult job market or location with few truly attractive options.

But whenever we are able to find and engage ourselves in satisfying and personally meaningful work, we increase our ability to live a full color life. Finding this work involves listening to ourselves: our passions, our gifts, and our strengths.

People discover their vocations in different ways. Some display such self-evident gifts that they seem to be on a clear path by elementary school. Many travel pinball-like journeys, pinging up and down multiple paths until finally stumbling upon one that fits. Some people build their careers on a well-considered assessment of their passions, interests, strengths and goals. Others faithfully follow a path of crumbs (positive experiences, fortuitous opportunities, encouragement, chance events) and ultimately stumble upon their destination.

Newspaper professional Sue VanDerzee is a great example of successful crumb-following. As a young woman, Sue was invited by a friend to join the staff of a community newspaper. Over time, finding success along the way, her responsibilities grew. She joined another paper, and now she serves as the editor.

Sue remembers:

> About this time I began thinking to myself, "This is all very fine, but what am I going to do when I grow up?" And I woke up one morning and I had this clear thought, this epiphany in my mind: "I'm doing what I love to do. What am I thinking? I'm a reporter, a journalist and editor, I'm making a contribution, I'm enjoying myself, I'm good at it — *this* is what I want to be when I grow up!"

Sue had believed that finding her right work had to be difficult. Instead, it had come her way. She explains the experience with this image: "My career seemed like a plant unfolding — like a flower."

Sue VanDerzee followed the trail of her interests and strengths into the field of publishing. Her advice:

> Try to choose a career that fits with your personality, both your strengths and your weaknesses. I'm best at starting things. I'm an enthusiastic person and I'm good in the beginning, but I wear out when things get repetitive. If I have to take an antibiotic for ten days, I will have completely forgotten it by the eighth day!! Which is why the newspaper business suits me; no two days are the same. Also, one of my weaknesses is that I have always been a procrastinator. I can't get away with that in a newspaper. The deadline forces me to get my work done — we don't put out blank pages.

Sometimes vocations change, yet the passions that fueled them remain. Megha has created a satisfying and successful career as teacher-trainer of yoga and Danskinetics®. In the process, she has largely left behind her earlier career as an actor. Yet she still finds ways to satisfy the passion that underlies her love of the theatre:

> I do miss acting, but don't miss the theatre lifestyle *at all.* I have found other ways of keeping theatre in my life. A few years ago I became a triple threat: producer, director, and actor in my own show of Eve Ensler's *The Vagina Monologues* in the very yoga center where I work! For me it was a great coup because although yoga has become my life, I will always and forever be an actress. But if I am to act, there must be an important message. *The Vagina Monologues* is exactly the kind of message I want to bring to the world: love of body, speaking the truth, being authentic. Performing the work of my heart

and soul onstage in front of hundreds of people was nothing short of Grace itself.

Another way I have brought theatre into my life of yoga is to remain open to interesting opportunities that arise. A director I know created an actors/writers workshop which truly fed my spirit. She had us write something important about our lives as women and then stand up and turn our writing into a theatre piece. The topics were not for the weak of heart! She would say, "Choose an animal and write its message to us humans about the state of the earth." We would write and then share what we had written. Once she said, "Write about your best sexual experience." With eyes bulging, we dutifully started writing. When it was time to read our pieces we all shouted, "We can't read this out loud, it's pornography!" But one by one we started, shamefully, to read. Hearing one another's stories along with our own was immensely powerful. We laughed, we cried, we saw and felt raw woman truth. As the months went by in these actor/writer workshops I thought, "I need no more theatre than this. If I can just keep this kind of raw expression, brilliance and self-expression through the word with like-minded people, that's enough for me.

Vocation is the active expression of our passions and gifts in the world. And while the themes remain consistent, over a lifetime the form will often change. Someone who is committed to teaching, for example, might find herself in several settings, working with a variety of people, over the course of a career. She may spend part of her career as a high school English teacher, then transition into an adult education program, then work in the training department of an organization; and perhaps later in life find an opportunity for service in teaching English to immigrant families.

The days of working in one job for an entire career are gone. More common will be enjoying three or more different careers over the course of our working lives.

FULL COLOR REFLECTION: VOCATION

If you are still trying to identify a vocational direction, think about our exploration so far. What clues have you uncovered about your personality, history, passions, gifts and strengths, and how they might direct you?

How would you describe your "deep gladness"?

Like Alicia, I suggest you narrow your focus to a direction that holds promise, then get moving and see what you find!

nine

THE PROMISE OF SURRENDER

We must be willing to let go of the life we have planned so as to have the life that is waiting for us.
Joseph Campbell

Another theme that emerged clearly from my interviews was the concept of surrender. Over and over I heard about the necessity to be able to surrender, welcome mystery, have trust, follow the lead of a source of guidance greater than ourselves. We can't make it all happen. In fact, often that is a good thing, because what we want to make happen may not be the best outcome for us.

The ego is not big on this surrender concept. And our society absolutely feeds into the belief that we need to be in control of our lives at all times. 'Plan the work, work the plan' directs us to establish goals, organize ourselves around the necessary tasks, and *execute!*

The assumption is that this is how responsible adults live. And of course we crave control — studies have shown that employees who display the most stress have the least control over their situations. Control makes us comfortable; the unknown, not so much.

Yet, experience confirms that the best laid plans often turn out very differently. And sometimes, when they turn out differently, we discover the gift at the end of an unexpected detour.

SURRENDER AND THE CLOCK

There are two words for time: *chronos* and *kairos*. Chronos is the standard sequential time that measures out our days. Our watches and our appointments are on chronological time.

Kairos is 'God's time' — the time that is right, ripe, ready, and appropriate. This time, of course, may have nothing to do with our beloved chronos. This time is not controllable. We need to be attuned to it, respond to it — but we can't manage it.

I will admit that I have an opinion about when things should happen. It is much easier to set goals and plan my life according to chronological time, rather than surrender and realize that I am living on God's time.

THE PROMISE OF SURRENDER

When I asked dolphin lady Marcia Mager what she thought was the biggest secret to full color living, she answered with one word: *surrender*. She explained:

> I'm slowly learning that if you just relax and surrender, you really can have what you want, although it might not exactly match what you think you want.
>
> If somebody truly surrenders, it is going to happen. You're surrendering to the Flow, God, the Universe, your Higher Self. You are surrendering to *what is*. That's the most advanced, evolved, spiritual stance anybody can take. It sounds simple, but it's not simple

to actually do it. We all want to control the shit out of everything.

Surrendering can feel like the most dangerous approach to life, because we are letting go of the fantasy that we are in control of everything. Surrender acknowledges the fact that we are part of a much larger whole. It doesn't mean giving up, but *allowing*.

One aspect of surrender relates to our external circumstances. Another form is surrender to the dynamics that are operating within us. It is the approach that most supports a clear connection between inner wisdom and outer action.

Surrender to inner prompting is the most reliable way to address those inconvenient realities that creep up on us and eventually demand our attention. For example, I may believe I should stay in this job or stay in this relationship or stay in this town, but something tells me change is afoot. Most of us want to hang on to the familiar, and we may do so to the cost of our happiness or health, increasing and prolonging the pain.

Surrender is simple, but not easy. It requires being willing to move into an unknown future. It goes against all our cultural norms of power, control, and order.

Surrender is ultimately an act of faith. In letting go, we find a blessing. We put ourselves in God's hands; release our tight hold on life, and take a step to real freedom.

EMBRACING THE MYSTERY

Letting go is made easier if we can rest in the mystery, not having a road map for exactly what will happen next. This comes more easily to some than to others.

Consultant Keith Merron says his wife definitely finds this easier than he does:

> I typically go into a situation wanting to understand and know it. My wife has the opposite tendency, gloriously wanting to connect to the mystery and all of its unknown.

There is something about being able to welcome the mystery in people who are living a fully expressed life.

It takes faith to make decisions that are guided by our inner wisdom, and then to rest in that mystery; almost as though life were a movie and we're waiting for the next scene.

My dear father was a man who embraced the mystery. Although he usually had clear goals for his actions, I believe he was tremendously entertained by watching to see what happened next.

After he passed away, I found this quotation written in his hand on his desk. He attributed it to the Oxford Group: "*Not only is today in God's keeping, but all our tomorrows; we have surrendered that to Him, too, so why fear whatever we think tomorrow might bring us? Fear of the future, whether it be tomorrow, or old age, means that we do not trust in God's guidance. Our faith in that future is the infallible test of our faith in Him.*"

Take a moment to look within. Have you been able to act on your inner wisdom and surrender to the future that follows, or are you still fighting for control, or trying to salvage a bad situation through force of will? It's not a question of who we should be or what we should do. Surrender involves acknowledging the truth of who we are and what we want, and being willing to follow the path that opens up before us.

PAIN AND RENEWAL

Ring the bells that still can ring.
Forget your perfect offering.
There is a crack in everything.
That's how the light gets in.
　　　　Leonard Cohen

One of my most challenging life experiences was the end of a 21-year marriage. I had always seen myself and my husband getting older together; retiring, traveling, and enjoying the grandchildren who would one day join our family.

Although the problems that ended our marriage certainly had developed over time, it seemed that very suddenly my envisioned future was gone. It was a shock. A friend of mine, who was also experiencing some difficult times, described her state to me: "The bike is operating with hitches in the gears, but at least it's moving forward." I replied, "Well, my chain fell off."

In the midst of the pain and confusion, I remember one thing was very clear. Although over my life I had experienced many challenges, this was my first major loss. With it, I had the sense that I had fully joined humanity.

Everyone has something that has broken their heart. We all have cracks in us. None of us gets through life without them.

Living a life in full color does not mean living without pain or loss. Many of the people I interviewed said their experiences of working through difficult times contributed to the fullness of their lives today.

Certainly, these are profound opportunities for learning and growth. We never invite them, but we recognize afterwards the value they brought. Author Elizabeth O'Connor points to the promise of these times: "When it seems to ourselves and to others that we are flying to pieces inside, it may be in order to integrate at a higher level of personality."[23]

How do people put the pieces back together? How do we find a state of wholeness after a shattering experience?

When my marriage ended, I had the uncommon experience of knowing not only what I needed to do to take care of myself, but how important it was that I do so. Being in crisis provides unusual clarity.

The first thing I did was reach out to family and friends and ask for their support. There were more than a few 2 AM phone calls during those first months.

The second step was to continue with individual counseling when couples' counseling no longer made sense. The third, and most unusual for me, was to have regular massages at a nearby massage therapy school's student clinic. I had an instinct that this could be of real value in my healing process. The fee was only $25, much more affordable than the fee for an experienced therapist; and massage addressed the need for pain release — and for touch — after my separation.

I also read books on separation and divorce. And, finally, in time, I forgave myself and my ex. All of these helped me navigate through a very difficult time.

For most of her adult life, Barb Wood has worked in the field of social service administration. Several major losses in her life propelled her into a period of change and growth, and today she is en route to a new career working with clients as a personal coach and yoga instructor.

Several years ago, within the space of just months, Barb's partner died after a three-year battle with cancer; Barb lost her job because of time away from work while taking care of her partner; her beloved elderly cat died, and she had a medical crisis. Any one of these constitutes a stressful event. Taken together, they add up to more than anyone should have to endure.

Barb says that in the midst of all the almost debilitating pain and loss, she was aware of the opportunity for growth it presented:

> Having gone through all of these losses, all at once, I felt I had to do a reboot on my life. For me, the experience of so much loss brought the recognition that even though it is extraordinarily painful, there was a blessing in it. I think this comes from Buddhist awareness and yoga practice — you don't often have an experience in life of everything emptying out at once.

No one would consciously choose to lose their partner, job, beloved pet and have a health crisis all at once. I had this acute awareness of the significance of that and really lived with that in as conscious a way as I could — so I avoided alcohol, continued to eat well, looked after my body, and I really focused on my spiritual practice.

Instead of filling up the void, I lived with the ambiguity of not knowing what's next, and allowed things to replace or fill in only when I knew they were really right. In time, I chose coaches training and yoga therapy training.

Over the last few years, I've been focused on healing and rebuilding and retooling myself for the next phase in my life, and now I feel ready to take the next step.

Barb's story brings to mind Elisabeth Kubler-Ross' comment: *"People are like stained-glass windows. They sparkle and shine when the sun is out, but when the darkness sets in, their true beauty is revealed only if there is a light from within."*

Experiences of pain and loss challenge us to find healthy and supportive ways to get through the period in one piece, and to see the gift that ultimately emerges. Often, these devastating experiences bring to light something that needs to change. Certainly they are often catalysts to a new level of understanding and wholeness.

FULL COLOR REFLECTION: PAIN AND RENEWAL

What has been your experience? How have you been held to the fire, emerging stronger, wiser, truer?

What experiences of pain or loss ultimately led to your new level of understanding and wholeness? Looking back, how have they contributed to the person you are today?

ten

BARRIERS TO FULL COLOR LIVING

Two dynamics make it very difficult for many of us to design a balanced life. We explored one of them earlier — the driven nature of today's society. We must always be on the go, accomplishing things. It can be hard to slow down, and almost impossible to come to a full stop.

The other is unrealistic and unhelpful expectations — expectations that to be a good or successful person, it is necessary to meet impossible standards of appearance, professional accomplishment, financial status, etc. Without clarifying for ourselves what are reasonable expectations, and defining for ourselves what a happy life looks like, we risk defaulting to the cultural norms.

In the next chapter, we'll explore some of the things we can do to support ourselves in living a full color life. First of all, we need to take a look at the society in which we are operating, and face these unrealistic and unhelpful expectations head-on.

OUR CONSUMER CULTURE

A client told his career counselor, "I've been living at the mercy of my résumé." He had been slowly progressing in his field, and although he no longer enjoyed the work, he was now too highly compensated to make a change without also significantly streamlining his lifestyle. With each promotion he was more trapped. He had a phrase for this conundrum: "biting the big biscuit" — making the Faustian bargain that promises more material reward, but with less freedom.

'Biting the big biscuit' is largely an unconscious response. A societally approved goal is presented to us, and we automatically chomp down on it. And if we have placed our sense of value in things, we continue to want more and better things. These things require money to buy and maintain, so we have a rather alarming self-reinforcing cycle on our hands.

Fortunately, it is possible to recognize the situation and change direction. As I write this, chiropractor Dean Nelson is about to leave with his wife and son on a three-year trip around the world. This is a rather nontraditional undertaking, yet Dean acknowledges that before he felt ready to let go of a traditional life, he felt the need to succeed on the world's terms.

Dean explains:

> I had to do the "gig": the successful practice, nice house, nice cars — some part of me was driven to be able to say "been there done that." So I achieved the bigger house, bigger practice, then I realized I didn't want to spend any more time learning those rules. The point of the game is to not continually succeed in the illusion; the point is to wake up.

Dieter Hannig is the German-born and internationally traveled Food & Beverage executive you met earlier. He believes the 'big biscuit' dynamics apply particularly to the North American lifestyle:

> There is a vicious cycle in America. People have big homes, big cars, big mortgages, big risks. Europeans are different — to us, big means waste. But giving something up, simplifying, doing with less — that all seems very counterintuitive to this North American culture.

What I see with friends and colleagues who live and work here is that a lot of them are hanging on to something they eventually realize has no true value. They are so busy working just to pay the bills; they don't even have time for relationships, for enjoying their lives.

Have you ever thought about the fact that we are called *consumers*? Is that what gives us value in our society? In the 18th century, there was a very different perspective: people thought of themselves as souls. They'd say, "She's a good soul." I find that far more appealing.

How do we disentangle ourselves from this consumer identity? One step is to recognize it for what it is — a manufactured and marketed image of what we should want in order to be happy and successful in our society. We can choose which part of this to accept, and which to ignore. Even better, we can consciously create goals for ourselves that are personally meaningful.

Does letting go of desiring the trappings of our consumer culture lead directly to full color living? Not entirely, or this would be a very short book! And I'm not suggesting that having a nice home, car, or state-of-the-art laptop is by definition a negative thing. These may represent the successful achievement of an important goal. What full color living requires, however, is a recognition that status and possessions do not define us, don't automatically make us happy, and should not reside at the top of our list of priorities.

EVALUATING EXPECTATIONS

Having addressed the impact of our consumer culture, let's dive further into the concept of expectations. These may be our expectations of ourselves, or others' expectations of us. The key to building a life that includes self-nurture and balance is to examine these expectations and make a conscious decision about which to keep, and which to heave out.

I was having lunch with my friend Joan, who is a successful professional with a Ph.D. in her field, a husband she adores, and a fulfilling life; in short, an intelligent and accomplished woman.

Our conversation turned to the topic of expectations. As a grown woman in her forties, Joan was still trying to address the fact that her parents, who live nearby, expected her to visit daily. Joan realized this was an unrealistic expectation and was trying to reduce her visits — to every *other* day!

We agreed that a good tool to help in situations like these would be a 'commitment audit.' What are the things you have committed yourself to, and why? Did you fall into these commitments, or did you make them consciously? Are there any that have outlasted their usefulness? Which do you choose to keep, and which are simply draining away time and energy from things in which you want to invest? In Joan's case, she wants to spend time with her parents, but she also needs to find a balance.

For Jay Wise, getting clear on expectations was central to his ability to enjoy his career and create a balanced life. Beyond his commitment to being an excellent dentist, Jay had to apply himself to mastering the art of running an office. He has always found the technical side of dentistry to be interesting and satisfying. However, managing a staff was far more challenging. (This is not uncommon for technical professionals whose field requires that they run a business and lead a staff.)

Jay talks about how he finally addressed his own unrealistic expectations:

> Early in my career, I wasn't good at setting boundaries. I was putting in long hours. I didn't delegate well, so I handicapped my staff's ability to help me. There was a time where I was more married to my dental practice than to my wife. It got to the point where I almost left the field — I thought, "This is going to kill me!" It was because I had

> unrealistic expectations. I held the inner belief that I should be able to do everything myself.
>
> Since then, I have invested a lot of time and energy in understanding myself better, learning how to become more effective in making a request, and in recognizing my own needs and boundaries. It's going much more smoothly and I enjoy what I'm doing.

Sometimes the expectations come from outside ourselves, such as a parent's desire for daily visits. Sometimes they come from within, such as Jay's belief that he should be able to do everything himself.

In her book, *Take Time for Your Life*, personal coach Cheryl Richardson takes on the commitment problem decisively. She suggests saying 'no' to everything that is not an absolute 'yes.'

> My basic coaching philosophy in working with clients is one of extreme self care — the foundation of a rich and fulfilling life. This means putting your self care above anything else — saying no unless it's an absolute yes, choosing to spend your time and energy on things that bring you joy, and making decisions based on what YOU want instead of what others want. . . you'll discover that when you start practicing extreme self care, a Divine force rallies behind you to support your decision and will actually make your life easier.[24]

What a radical idea this seemed when I first ran across Cheryl's book (which has become quite dog-eared and marked up from use in the years since I discovered it.) Here was a personal coach, hired to help people build successful, satisfying lives, and she is suggesting that rather than begin with adding things, they should *subtract*.

The first task is to identify and remove those commitments and expectations that do not support what's really important. In that way, we make space in time, energy and resources for what is.

Another approach is to become clear about our priorities up front. In the early days of his career, Dan Brewer, who today is a lawyer in private practice, decided to hire a career coach and enter into a conscious self assessment and goal identification process. The result:

> My coach Jan, was a helpful mirror. She gave me an opportunity to explore my approach to work, my beliefs about values, money, etc. I had to sort out my attitudes and definitions about success and failure.
>
> I discovered I could define success for myself. It didn't have to be defined by billable hours, or perceived ranking, or some other industry norm. I realized I don't have to log 2,200 billable hours a year. I have the freedom to keep my professional work in perspective.
>
> Today I have a successful private practice that allows me professional scope and intellectual engagement, and I love the flexibility. If I need to stay in the office late to work on a brief, so be it. On the other hand, if the opportunity presents itself that I can take an afternoon off and go sailing, I'll do that.

Dan's story is another example of identifying and challenging automatic assumptions. Particularly in a traditional field such as law, where expectations have been laid down through the ages, it requires conscious decision making to fashion a career that will be ultimately satisfying.

Dan could have easily bought into the 'work long hours, make a name for yourself and get that corner office' frame of mind. Instead, he has a flourishing private practice, a balanced family life, and a healthy perspective on full color living: on a sunny summer day, you may find him sailing in Massachusetts Bay rather than sitting at his computer.

Newspaper editor Sue VanDerzee has long recognized that tradeoffs are required in order to have time for the things that are important to her:

> I really don't care about housework. It's legendary in my family. My husband does more than I do.
>
> As we get older, I think it becomes easier to take all those expectations — "I should be able to keep the house clean *and* run the newspaper *and* see my friends *and* spend time with my family" — and say, "*No, I can't.*" Then you have to know what your values are so you make your choices and you feel okay about them. It really doesn't matter to me about having a clean kitchen if there is a grandchild to hug or an article to write.

Clearly, expectations and priorities are linked. Sue's priorities are clear, and she is able to dismiss expectations that she feels are less important. How does your use of time reflect your own priorities? Are there expectations you need to set aside in order to focus on what is most important to you today?

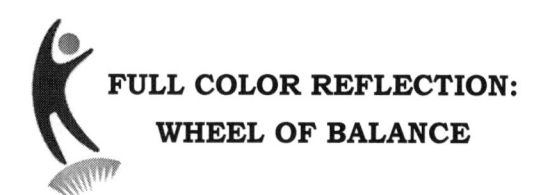

FULL COLOR REFLECTION: WHEEL OF BALANCE

Here's a simple exercise that can help you see how your time and energy are being invested today.

On the wheel of balance on the next page, rate each area on your current level of satisfaction. Draw a point close to the center if you are very dissatisfied; mark a point at the outer edge of the circle if you are completely satisfied. And of course, if you're somewhat satisfied, pick a spot somewhere between the two.

When you have plotted your level of satisfaction for each of the eight dimensions, draw a line connecting all the dots. See how even or uneven it appears.

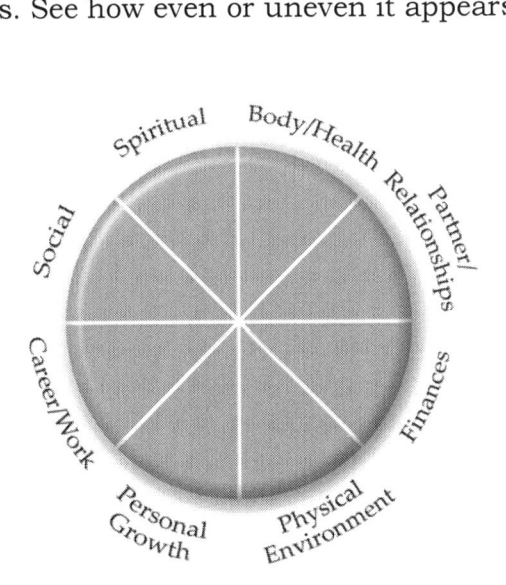

(Wheel diagram with eight dimensions: Spiritual, Body/Health, Partner/Relationships, Finances, Physical Environment, Personal Growth, Career/Work, Social)

In which areas do you experience the greatest satisfaction? There's something to celebrate!

In which areas do you see the greatest opportunity for improvement? If you were to choose just one of these areas to make changes, which would it be, and what would you do?

Life is a constant process of adjustment and fine tuning. We get one part sorted out, and immediately another demands our attention. Sometimes we need to accept periods of imbalance — such as when a big project is due at work, or a family member requires most of our time and attention. We simply need to make sure the imbalance doesn't become a permanent condition.

Creating a balanced life is an ongoing process, and it begins with awareness and a commitment to taking steps to bring our life in alignment with our values, priorities, and desires.

eleven

NURTURING A FULL COLOR LIFE

SELF CARE

At the end of a yoga class I take each week, one of the women commented that women tend to put their needs last. There was immediate agreement all around. (This happens to be a yoga class whose members are all women — men are welcome, but only one has braved the class, and he didn't stay long.) What I found interesting was how strongly everyone agreed about this issue. At the same time, don't the men in our lives also feel that they are often juggling more than they can handle?

You just took a look, using a simple pie chart, at your level of satisfaction in eight key areas of your life. Several of these areas can be enhanced through self care. Self care is how we attend to our physical, emotional, mental, and spiritual needs so that we are able to live a fully expressed life. This may include a workout regimen, seeking out counseling during a difficult period, finding work that provides an opportunity for ongoing learning, getting out into nature, time spent in quiet contemplation. . . and the yoga class I just mentioned.

The trick with self care is to ensure it is built into our lives, and not left as a 'nice to have' once all our responsibilities have been discharged. We all know that the 'to do' list is a lifelong project — complete one task, add two more; you never reach the end.

Too many people (and I have certainly been guilty of this) wait until they are completely burned out by taking care of chores, jobs, family duties, and the expectations of others. Only then do they realize that they have neglected themselves and are suffering the consequences.

As we get older, we lose the resilience that enabled us to (dysfunctionally) burn out all cylinders and still keep moving. We learn that we need to reprioritize and put our self care at the top of the list.

TAKING BREAKS

It took me many years to figure out that we are built to work in natural cycles — times of activity, times of rest. Times of rest feed our bodies, minds and spirits, making those times of activity most productive and creative. Author Brenda Ueland spoke to the need for downtime as a source of creative inspiration: *"Imagination needs noodling — long, inefficient, happy idling, dawdling and puttering."*

What lovely words — *idling, dawdling, puttering;* so goal free; so liberating. They give us permission — encouragement, even — to take a break and just be. If we don't have the wits about us to find time to take these needed breaks, there are real consequences. We find ourselves burned out, sick, depressed, depleted, unproductive, and ill-tempered. Not a happy picture.

I remember one particularly stressful period, when I had a small business and two young children at home. My business was growing, and I was running on all cylinders without any down time.

One of my clients was a hospital system. During a particularly busy period, while walking through a hospital ward after conducting an interview, I remember looking longingly at a crisp white empty bed and thinking, "If only I could stay for a few days." How pathetic is that?! Clearly, I had not found a way to balance my needs with those of my business and family.

How do you recognize the need to take a break, before reaching that stressed state? It's not always easy. Karen Van Dyke, who works at a corporate banking office, describes her moment of realization:

> We have motion sensors in our offices that control the overhead lights. I was working at my computer, and all of a sudden the lights went off. It's a shock. You think, "You idiot! That means you've sat for an hour and 15 minutes *without moving!*" Isn't that a great visual? When that happened, I freaked, then I thought, that's God's way of saying "Do something other than sitting there addicted to the emails!"

Some people need to be reminded to rest, others are more self-aware and know when they need a pause in their day. Food and beverage executive Dieter Hannig says:

> When I need to step away from the office, I walk outside and sit on a bench for 20 minutes. I just look at the clouds and do some breathing exercises. I don't schedule this, but I do it; you have to have time for yourself.

The great artist Leonardo Da Vinci recommended times of rest to gain perspective:

> Every now and then go away, have a little relaxation, for when you come back to your work your judgment will be surer since to remain constant at work will cause you to lose power of judgment. Go some distance away because then the work appears smaller and more of it can be taken in at a glance and a lack of harmony and proportion is more readily seen.

Building in times for rest is the most reliable way to ensure self care. It may be 30 minutes in the morning for some meditation or stretching, a Saturday morning sleep-in ritual, evening strolls, or simply stepping out of the office and into the fresh air for a quick, mind clearing break.

FULL COLOR REFLECTION: TAKE A BREAK

What kinds of breaks do you find most refreshing?

What kinds of breaks can you easily fit into your day?

What would help you create more time and opportunity for rest and renewal?

CARING FOR OUR BODY AND SPIRIT

People who want to live a full color life find ways to look after themselves. What works best differs for each person. Regardless of the approach, they are able to let go of that constant identification with mind (or career, or achievement, identity, or whatever is wrapping you around that familiar pole), and give attention to the body and the spirit.

Hospital chaplain Peter Lund has discovered the practice of Tai Chi:

> It helps clear my mind so I can become aware of my body's functioning, of breathing, and moving. It takes me out of my focus on my roles — trying to be the 'best father' or the 'best worker.'
>
> Just this awareness of being in my body has been immensely helpful. I spend too much time in my head. Tai Chi grounds me and helps me listen to my body. Through this

practice, I am calmer and more supportive at home, and more effective at work.

Restaurant marketing vice president Jill Ramsier is a true believer in 'healthy mind/healthy body.' Regular exercise keeps her fit and strong, and it allows her some mental space:

> I work out regularly, usually five days a week. That is a big part of my life because if I didn't, I'd feel pushed on the edge a bit. Some people meditate, some people practice yoga, I work out — that's when I let my mind kind of veer off and take a break.

Therapist Michael Brown sees physical wellbeing as a pre- requisite to effectiveness in his work:

> My commitment is to the service of my clients, and in order to do that I have to be in peak shape. Here's how I organize my life: I always get eight hours' sleep; I never don't. I also take a 20-minute nap in the middle of the afternoon. I exercise regularly — three days a week at least. I do everything it takes for me to be fully attentive 100% of the time to each client.

Barb Wood practices yoga daily as a discipline for wellbeing. She also found yoga to be a source of comfort during a time of crisis in her life:

> When a series of major losses hit at once, I made a decision to go to as many yoga classes as I wanted to for several months.

> I wasn't able to do much of a personal practice at that time. I could barely move some days, but I experienced my yoga mat as a place of solace and salvation. I really feel this was such a beneficial thing, to keep coming back, coming back, coming back to that center, that knowing, peaceful place.

Yoga and dance instructor Megha advises that whatever you do:

Move your body! When I'm working with my yoga and movement students, my goal is to get them into their bodies. Many people walk around this earth as if their bodies are there simply to make their heads portable. My job is to interrupt that and give them the gift of an embodied life.

Today I'll be teaching my signature piece, "*Let Your Yoga Dance: Grace in Motion*," which blends both yoga and user-friendly dance in a noncompetitive way. At the end of the hour the students will be significantly different. This is an express route to joy. They see there is another way to live inside themselves. They see that they are all dancers. That is my mission: to make everyone in our sick, sad culture understand that our birthright is that we are dancers, one and all.

I can't write about self care without noting the fact that physical exercise and nutrition are vital components of a healthy life — but you know that. One fact you may not know is that almost all the cells in our bodies — and we have trillions of them — are constantly replacing themselves at a rate of about 1% per day.

Basically, we get a new body every three months — and we have a choice whether it will be a decaying, aging body, or a vibrant one. A healthy lifestyle — including regular exercise and good nutrition — creates healthier, stronger cells, building a body that is ready to fully take on life.[25]

There are other sources of self-care that stretch different aspects of the self — the mind and spirit. For example, taking a class in a subject you've always been interested in. Developing hobbies such as photography, art, or woodworking. Playing in a band or singing with a choir. Taking in the current exhibit at the art gallery or science museum. Learning a language or joining a book club. Picking up an interest that was abandoned when the *real world* demanded our attention.

Look for those experiences that nourish your soul and bring you joy. Take steps to make room for them and welcome them. Then, see how magnificently they enrich your life.

A SIMPLER LIFE

Ordinary is good. Ordinary and wonderful are what life is.
                                              Roger Housden

In the midst of a culture that seems to celebrate excess and idolize consumption, it was interesting to hear from those I interviewed that one of the elements of a full color life is the ability to enjoy the simple things. This obviously provides more flexibility — if you are happy with less, your range of choices is far greater. But it also speaks to the ability we discussed earlier, of being able to live in the present and appreciate what is right in front of us.

The default in our culture is to increase the complexity of life. When I was growing up, many of my uncles and aunts were farmers in Canada. Their days revolved around running the farm, feeding the family, attending church services, and I imagine ordering supplies and paying bills.

There were no computers, no cell phones. They didn't even have their own phone lines; they had shared 'party lines.' I am sure much has changed in the farming business, but I remember my farming relatives as being calm, unhurried and able to enjoy their family lives.

Simple, unremarkable things and unadorned moments can be sources of joy. A simpler life can be liberating.

SUPPORTIVE STRUCTURE

We've touched on the value of setting priorities and ensuring that we allocate time for the things that mean the most to us. Another approach to creating a simple and satisfying life is through structure. Some people may find this too confining, but psychiatrist Jack Weltner uses structure as a strategy to ensure he devotes his time to what he values most. Over the years, he has perfected his approach:

> Much of my life is structured. I go to the office or the clinic at 8, come home at 6. I basically wear the same clothes: one of my turtleneck sweaters, pants, and the same shoes. I exercise three times a week and I know exactly when that will be. All that makes life simple.
>
> I don't have to put a lot of energy into planning, and that gives me freedom. And this isn't just about creating time for obligations — I've always set aside time to meet friends for lunch because I love having lunch with people. I leave two hours in the middle of the workday, and that is on my schedule, several days every week. It works for me.

Paradoxically, structure provides Jack with an increased sense of freedom and the ability to enjoy a rich and fulfilling life.

FULL COLOR REFLECTION: SELF-CARE

What forms of self care work for you? Aerobics, tai chi, yoga, sports, walking, and other physical disciplines all contribute to self care. They're all good; the goal is to find one or more that work for you and make them a priority in your daily life.

Do you include self care in your life on a regular basis? How?

Is there anything you want to change, delete or add in order to ensure you are caring for your body and spirit?

twelve

FULL COLOR RELATIONSHIPS

THE IMPORTANCE OF RELATIONSHIPS

One of the joys of working on this book has been reconnecting with old friends and gaining their insight. One friend and I discovered we had traveled very similar journeys in the 30 years since we had last seen each other. She described to me the end of one marriage and the discovery of a new, more supportive partnership. It was great to hear that she was so happy. In speaking about her husband, she celebrated the comfort of knowing there is someone who cares, who always 'has your back.'

We live in relationship. There are some who prefer solitude and their own company, but most of us yearn to share ourselves and live our lives in relationship with others.

One day I happened to catch the National Press Club's luncheon on TV. The keynote speaker was well known economist, lawyer, author, professor, film and television performer and overall smart guy, Ben Stein.

I was expecting a speech about economics, but what followed was quite different. Here, in sum, was Ben Stein's advice: "The best investment you can make, better than stocks, bonds, or money markets, is in spending time with your kids."

Our families of origin are assigned to us; these are our first key relationships. Other relationships emerge organically through our interactions in school, work, and other activities. Beyond that, we may need to take conscious action to develop the relationships we are seeking.

Whether it be children, partners, extended family or friends, happy and healthy relationships are key to our well-being. Healthy relationships require nurturing. This means putting a priority on time invested in our relationships, and sometimes leaving our comfort zone in order to create opportunities for new relationships to develop.

Hospital chaplain Peter Lund believes that we all have three kinds of relationships, and they are deeply connected: to ourselves, to others, and to God. Understanding one can illuminate the others.

Peter's awareness of the importance of relationships in his life was sparked during graduate school:

> It was the end of a romance in my twenties that led me to an exploration of my self — my inner life. Then I realized that if I understood something about my relationship to my parents, that told me something about my relationship to God. As I explored what I believe about God, I started learning things about relationship.
>
> Becoming aware of the power of relationships, becoming more skilled in having healthy relationships, has been huge in my life, and I would say that taking time to look at and to work at relationships is a central part of living fully.

We don't always know which relationships will become important through lines in our lives. English and publishing professor David Emblidge spoke about his friendship with three buddies who have been close since college:

> These friendships have turned out to be deeply rewarding. Over the years, they've deepened in a herky jerky manner, but when they move

forward they really move forward! I've never failed these friends and they haven't failed me. And we have been there for each other through health concerns where each of us had to stare the end-game issues in the face. I feel blessed to have these three amazing people in my life.

There is a particular magic in a close friendship with someone who knows us well. It is a blessing to have one or two trusted friends with whom we can talk, laugh, commiserate, and, in my case, take a long, chatty walk. When I lived in Marblehead, Massachusetts, my friend Cathie Michaud and I regularly walked about three miles to the harbor and back, happily gabbing all the way. We enjoyed the exercise plus the ear of a good and helpful friend.

Strong relationships can help us become more powerfully ourselves. I love this quote by Sally Kempton, which I ran across in the Yoga Journal: *"There is no faster way to elevate your consciousness than hanging around with someone who knows who he or she is and who you are, and who won't let you get away with being anything less."*

Creating and maintaining nurturing and enjoyable relationships requires time and some effort. They don't always happen automatically, and they're not always easy. But it's worth the investment; a strong network of healthy relationships benefits all of us—body, mind, and spirit.

BEING PART OF A COMMUNITY

When my kids were young, we lived in Stockbridge, Massachusetts, and attended the First Congregational Church in that charming western Massachusetts town. A weekend family retreat was scheduled and we decided to go. This would be a new adventure.

The theme of the retreat was the Congregational Church's conference theme of the year — our relationship to money. On the face of it, this could have been a very dry topic. I soon discovered that it provided an entry point to an opportunity for profound community.

Over the course of the weekend, we explored the concept of money and our relationships with it; we gathered in the evenings for discussions, and broke into small groups to delve further. We also prepared and shared meals, played with the children, brought out the guitars, danced, enjoyed the outdoors, and had a lot of fun.

For me, this retreat was a life changing experience, because instead of the standard coffee hour small talk, we were sharing important parts of ourselves, our perspectives, our histories. I was having conversations with people I had known socially, but now, for the first time, I was being given a far more complete and engaging picture of who they were.

The author Thomas Moore refers to this deep level of contact with others: *"We need people in our lives with whom we can be as open as possible. To have real conversation with people may seem like such a simple, obvious suggestion, but it involves courage and risk."*[26]

I found this retreat experience somewhat frightening initially, but also tremendously rewarding. For me, it provided an eye-opening experience — it demonstrated the value of being able to engage in deep, thoughtful conversations with others. It showed me the value of real contact in community.

Our communities can also provide acknowledgment and support for who we are and what we do. We see ourselves and our abilities reflected back from others.

Ideally, this reflection will be accurate and supportive, not influenced or complicated by others' agendas or issues. The artist Greg Mort first discovered that he had a special talent while in elementary school. He recalls:

> I was always the best drawer in class. My friends would constantly ask me to draw pictures of things for them. When that happens to a person over and over, that becomes who you are — "oh that's him; he's the artist."
>
> They enable you. It took me years to really accept it. Even after I started selling my work

and making some money, people would say, "You're the artist!" and I'd say, "I guess."

Greg also believes that the positive response he received from others was key in ultimately pursuing his art:

> I worked at it in part because I received a positive response from others. Let's say I was five years old and was doing some really cool drawings and nobody said anything about it, or they said that's terrible, that would have affected me and maybe I would have pursued something else.
>
> To this day, I take pleasure in hearing people's response to my work. It's something human beings need. My dog wants to constantly be reassured she's a good dog. It feels good to hear you're a good dog. I love hearing it. Maybe in time you grow tired of that, but I certainly haven't.

It was interesting for me to hear Greg describe the value of reinforcement. Over the years I have had the opportunity to see the art he creates, and I am so impressed and moved by his ability and the beautiful paintings. Yet, having accomplished so much, Greg still describes that very human (and canine!) need for feedback that we all share. In relationships we see ourselves, and our gifts, reflected in the eyes of others.

One of the great things about communities is that we can join them or build them ourselves. Matchmaker Lanie Delphin says:

> After an unhappy marriage of 30 years, I finally realized that my happiness would have to come from me and what I made of my life. I learned how to build community and give and take what I needed.
>
> Becoming an active member of the Beyond War peace movement when I was in my 30s gave me a confidence I never had, a sense that

I could make a difference, that I could change people's minds and help inspire them.

Community is the setting in which we can be in service to others. This provides meaning and purpose beyond our individual lives and achievements. Editor Sue VanDerzee notes:

> More important than the day-to-day stuff is the impact we can have — the way that people working together can make life better for everybody. You know — form communities, heal the sick, feed the hungry, stop the wars — all that good stuff.

Over the course of a life, we create our communities. They may include family, friends, co-workers, and other fascinating connections. They may reach back to kindergarten, or include a relationship that began today.

Our communities provide us support and an opportunity to contribute. They may all congregate together, or may be a dispersed group of people from a variety of locations. They may be a homogeneous group (like *all my high school friends*), or a crazy quilt of people we've stitched into our lives over time. Either way, it's your community.

One time I had occasion to call my community into active service. I was interviewing for a job I really wanted and needed. On the way to the interview from the parking lot, I thought of using visualization to call my community in to help. (Some people would call in their angels, or guides, it's all good.)

I thought about people who were supportive of me and my work. I quickly jotted down a list of 14 people — colleagues, family, friends, clients, and teachers. I named them My Parade. Then, as I walked from the parking lot to the interview, I imagined them following in a row behind me. I called each of their names out loud, and invited the entire entourage to follow me in to the interview and help me land this job. Which they did, and I did.

THE COMMUNITY AT WORK

It was years ago, in my early experiences of spending time in organizations, that I came up with the concept of living a gray life. Too often, whether in a hospital, school, insurance agency, bank, retailer, whatever the industry — I saw people who were presumably being paid 100% of their salary, clearly bringing maybe 50% of themselves into work.

I knew even then that this wasn't simple obstinacy or laziness on their part. There was something about the work environment that didn't call out their full participation. Several decades later, the overall situation is little changed, as I have seen during my years working in organizations, both as an employee and external consultant.

One friend who works in a traditional corporate job evoked a lot of emotion and descriptive imagery when asked to describe the experience of being in her work community:

> In my company, it's definitely gray. It's very difficult to keep your color when you are being bombarded — it's like a constant laser game the kids play, getting shot at all the time. . . Last year it was like a cyclone every day . . . I see how hard the people on my team try, without the resources they need, the changes they have to go through while at the same time trying to build a business. It's like the management are in the chariot, whipping the stallions who are pulling it . . .

Yikes. Certainly it is not like this everywhere, yet in the standard surveys of job satisfaction, the majority will consistently report that they are unhappy with their jobs. Clearly there is room for improvement here. Why do companies, especially large companies, tend to be so inhospitable to full color living?

One of the problems with organizational life derives from the structure of the organizations themselves. As author and consultant Geoffrey Bellman outlines in his book, *The Consultant's Calling*, organizations operate through rigid structures created not to support people, but to follow a mechanistic worldview. In his opinion:

> We have lost the 'organ' in organization as we have built awkward hierarchical structures with boxes and lines connecting. Consider the sister words to *organization*, such as *organ, organism, and organic* (not to mention *orgasm* and *orgy*); these words are filled with life! Instead of creating rich, life filled, working organisms, too often we have created structures modeled after machines — mechanistic, sharply defined, and inflexible — that force their moving human parts to act like machines too.[27]

Adding to the problem, these organizations tend to value only one part of the worker-as-machine. Especially in traditional white collar environments, organizations want employees to bring their minds and, if possible, not much more.

Author and consultant Keith Merron continues the theme:

> Businesses are designed to produce a profit. Their structure and processes are considered the primary vehicles for success, and people and their spirit are often asked to subordinate themselves. This worldview tends to reinforce structured thinking, and the intellect itself.
>
> In order to succeed in this environment, people have to cut off parts of themselves. They are not invited to bring their whole selves to work, just their intellects.
>
> But an interesting pattern is emerging. As the world is getting more unstable, changing more and at an increasing rate, the standards of predictability, reliability and repeatability are no longer sources of success. We're perhaps the first generation to rethink the old model. What's exciting is that in order to succeed in the new environment, we can't just rely on the

intellect; we've got to embrace more fully all of ourselves.[28]

Times are a-changing. *Fast Company Magazine* regularly features stories about companies that are moving away from machine-like operations and towards something more humane. These emerging organizations are built around values that promote both individual satisfaction and organizational achievement.

With good talent growing increasingly scarce, and younger generations unwilling to put up with the artificial structure and unrealistic expectations of their elders, companies are being forced to make themselves more attractive. This requires addressing the needs of the entire person, and not seeing their employees merely as parts of the corporate machine.

The author, David Whyte, sounded the call for a more inclusive view in his book, *The Heart Aroused*:

> Institutions must now balance the need to make a living with a natural ability to change. They must also honor the souls of the individuals who work for them and the great soul of the natural world from which they take their resources.[29]

Historical changes that brought us the industrial revolution created the hierarchical structures we know so well. Global changes, including scientific advancements, technology, governments, economics, and the physical environment are demanding that the old structure shifts.

Even our understanding of the nature of reality challenges the existing order. The field of science, particularly Quantum Theory, has demonstrated that we are primarily made of energy, not solid matter, and that we are all connected through this energy — not standing alone as separate units of matter. How does that impact our understanding of what organizations should and can be?

This is an exciting time of change. Organizations will need to continue to transition to new ways of being. They will need to be more supportive of including the whole person at work, if they are to compete successfully for talent and for business. Further, as we work with the changing paradigm, we have the opportunity to create organizations that can truly fulfill the potential they hold as thriving centers of community, meaning and contribution.

Let me bring in a topic we discussed earlier because it also applies here. The common practice of focusing on and trying to improve individual weaknesses as a way of developing employees has been challenged by those who believe that our strengths hold our greatest potential. As organizations embrace the view that it is in their interest to help employees identify and make the most of their strengths — and as individuals take responsibility for helping their organizations do just that — we will naturally move toward workplaces that embrace the whole person.

In the meantime, what can you do if you are unhappily stuck in an old paradigm organization? If you don't see healthy changes emerging, get out. That's the ideal option. There are organizations — a smaller number, but they exist — that offer environments that are welcoming of the whole person. Leave where you are, find one of these, or join the increasing ranks of entrepreneurs and create one yourself.

If that is not possible at this time, then make a conscious decision to stay, and be at peace with that decision. Don't allow yourself to be a victim; that drains energy and makes it completely impossible to live in full color.

In this case, do what many people do — look for ways to bring more of yourself to work and life within whatever parameters you have. Seek out friendships with like-minded people. Take breaks, get out for a walk during lunch; do what you can to support your wellbeing. Use your time away from work to ensure that you feed the other needs you have — for creativity, for physical activity, for intellectual stimulation, for fun, for quiet and rest. Along the way, you may begin to see a subtle shift in your organization, as companies continue their transition to a new, more inclusive and conscious way of being.

EXPRESSION

thirteen

FULL COLOR LIVING

*Don't ask what the world needs.
Ask what makes you come alive, and do it. Because what
the world needs is people who have come alive.*

Howard Thurman, Theologian

BEING TRUE TO YOURSELF BRINGS JOY

We've been on quite a journey so far, exploring full color living in all its dimensions. We've recognized our many identifications, both internal and external, and seen that we each have a reliable, wise center that is connected to spiritual wisdom. That center is the point from which all full color living emerges.

Besides working to understand our personalities better, we also celebrate that we each have a unique, quirky, colorful set of inner characters and issues that both help and hinder us.

But the goal is not to transcend our personalities. We can't say, "Okay, I'm just going to be pure soul energy from now on." Goofy and challenging as they may be, our personalities are the instruments our souls need for expression.

We've talked about some things that can support us in identifying and strengthening our center, such as meditation and self care. We've looked at passions, gifts, strengths and vocations — what we love, what we're good at, what we want and need to do.

And we have talked about the dynamics of full color living — of living in present time, being open to growth and exploration, surrendering to what is, and ensuring that we live in nurturing relationship to others.

Along the way, you've encountered opportunities for *Full Color Reflection* — exercises designed to help you apply the concepts of full color living to the circumstances of your own life. Some of these exercises may have provided straightforward data; others may have offered surprising or profound new insights.

Hopefully there have been some helpful reminders in these pages about who you really are, what is ultimately important to you, and what you want in your life. You may have identified some changes you'd like to make. Now it's time to look at how we bring this knowledge into expression in the world.

One principle I came across regularly as I researched this book — taken from ancient philosophers, self help authors, and the people I interviewed, was this: *Being true to yourself brings joy.*

So how do we do that? How do we act in ways that are true to ourselves? And what happens when we do?

First, listen. Remember the center we've been talking about so often? That wise core, that connection to spirit, is your listening post for authentic action. It bears repeating: it is often difficult to listen to what we know is true for ourselves when there are so many competing messages — from those voices within, and from our families, friends and society. Your center is your reliable source of guidance, so listen.

Then, act. Life may not happen the way we expect, but nothing will happen unless we act. By acting, we give God something to work with. We make our intentions known. We become co-creators with God, and life becomes a work of art.

Personal coach Cheryl Richardson promises:

> When you live your life based on your inner wisdom, your Wise Self, you come to realize that the life you thought you wanted was only the beginning. A Divine power takes over, and as you listen to and act on your inner wisdom, you're guided to a life beyond your wildest dreams.

I think the life Cheryl refers to is "beyond your wildest dreams" because it is uniquely *your life*. And because when we are true to ourselves, we release so much energy that we see, maybe for the first time, that our expectations have been far too limited.

FULL COLOR REFLECTION: BEING TRUE TO MYSELF

Before we go further, let me remind you of the story of Marcia and the dolphins. Marcia had a tremendous passion about something, yet couldn't take action until finally she was able to accept the truth and act on it.

I wonder if, in the course of reading this book, something has emerged for you, just as strong as Marcia's desire about dolphins. It may be something that is standing between you and being true to yourself.

It may have to do with a passion you have not allowed yourself to explore, even as a hobby.

It may have to do with some aspect of your life — your relationships, work, lifestyle, environment, or location — where you are settling for something other than what you really want.

It may have to do with who you really are, what you really want, or both.

It may be something that, if acknowledged, would require a change. As we've said before, most of us have frighteningly high thresholds for pain before we finally succumb to the press for authenticity.

Is there something that is holding you back from being true to yourself? If so, can you think of a safe, healthy, nurturing way to take a step toward greater authenticity? This can be frightening, yet it yields great rewards. Even a small step in the right direction puts you on the road to wholeness.

DIRECTING OUR ENERGY

As I write this, *The Secret* has been at the top of the New York Times nonfiction bestseller list for 84 weeks. *The Secret* explores the *law of attraction*, which suggests that we create the circumstances of our lives through our thoughts, emotions and beliefs, and that we can actively participate in bringing more of what we want into our lives.

Conversely, according to this universal law, we — sometimes unconsciously — may also attract more of what we don't want. For example, if we are complaining about always being broke, we will continue to be broke, because that's where our attention and emotions are focused. The premise of the law of attraction suggests that the universe doesn't discriminate between an energetic message about what we do want or what we don't want; it will deliver on whatever message is sent.

Yet the basic principles in *The Secret* are not new. First of all, they summarize work of others who have written about the law of attraction, including Esther and Jerry Hicks, whose Abraham Teachings have articulated these concepts for over a decade.

But we can look further back for the ancestry of these teachings. Napoleon Hill, who published *Think and Grow Rich* over 60 years ago, saw a direct relationship between what we focus on and the results we get. Hill said, *"The most powerful instrument we have in our hands is the power of our mind."* Hill also made the connection between mind and emotions: *"Desire is the starting point of all achievement, not a hope, not a wish, but a keen pulsating desire which transcends everything."*

Many have built on Hill's foundation, including Earl Nightingale, Anthony Robbins, and others in the personal success field. They intuitively understood that the power of the mind could deliver concrete results. What has changed in the intervening years is our understanding of the nature of reality and of how that can be true.

Fascinating breakthroughs have been made since my days in high school physics, when we were studying the properties of protons, neutrons and electrons. Since then, scientists have discovered that we — and our surroundings — are not composed of solid matter, even though we appear solid. Instead, we are far more open space than matter; we are primarily energy, moving so quickly as to appear solid.

We are energy. We interact with others through that energy. You've experienced this. You can tell whether someone gives you energy or is an energy drain. You sense when a situation is taxing to your spirits, or life-promoting. You don't need any special equipment or talent, you just know. You resonate or don't resonate with something or someone. It feels right, or it doesn't. You pick up these energetic cues naturally.

Further — and here's where the concepts of the law of attraction become more than theory — how we direct our energy impacts our lives. We tend to attract what we give our energy to.

Again, this is probably easiest to see in the negative. Most of us know someone who is constantly complaining about a life issue — an unhappy relationship, or money troubles, or a health concern. And the more the person complains, the more tightly the problem seems to hold on.

The author Sarah Ban Breathnach describes this common situation:

> Many of us unconsciously create drama in our minds, expecting the worst from a situation only to have our expectations become a self fulfilling prophesy. Inadvertently we become

> authors of our own misfortune. And so we struggle from day to day, from crisis to crisis, bruised and battered by circumstances without realizing that we always have a choice . . .
>
> What if you began to expect the best from any situation? Isn't it possible that you could write new chapters in your life with happy endings? Suspend your disbelief. Take a leap of faith. After all, what have you got to lose but misery and lack?[30]

The struggles and crises experienced by people with a negative view aren't likely that person's conscious goal, but they are the result nonetheless. What if we were instead to direct our attention and emotions toward those things we *do* want to include in our lives?

Marcia Mager shares her approach:

> Whenever I'm at a low in my life something happens, I guess because I have a tremendous desire for it to happen. I think about it, I talk about it, I pray about it, I journal about it, I make my desire conscious. I ask. That's part of the secret. I specifically ask the universe, and I ask with a tremendous heart.

Visualization is a tool commonly used to connect with inner knowing. It can also be used to focus energy towards something that is wanted.

Whether done purposefully, or as a natural habit of keeping intended goals front and center, visualization helps people clarify and focus on their goals: not what they don't want, but what they do.

Visualization is not magic. Its value is in focusing and directing attention so that we can clearly see what we want to bring into our lives — and apply our energy accordingly. And I'm not just talking about material things here, but all aspects of a full color life — meaningful work, thriving relationships, healthy bodies, beautiful environments, fun experiences . . . the whole enchilada.

As we focus on what we want to bring into our lives, we begin to see more opportunities. They were probably always there, but now they have our attention.

FULL COLOR REFLECTION: CREATING A TREASURE MAP

One exercise I do every few years is to create a visual treasure map. This is a physical, concrete way to apply the principles of the law of attraction — by identifying and giving energy to what we want to attract into our lives now. This is also a fun exercise to do with a group of friends.

There are many ways to go about creating your treasure map, but the main idea is to find or create images of what you want to bring more of into your life. Some time spent looking through magazines or sifting through internet images will provide plenty of material. You can also create images by hand. What kind of pictures will you choose?

One friend created a treasure map in which she included pictures of people happily engaged in sports and exercise, because she wanted to become physically stronger and more agile. Another chose a picture of a handsome looking fellow, because she was ready to attract a relationship into her life. Another gravitated to pictures that represented a peaceful life, as she had gone through a troubling period and was ready for a break. Another wanted to make a career change and chose images that represented her intended new work. Your goal is to choose what is meaningful and attractive to you *at this point in your life*.

It is helpful to be as open minded as possible while doing this exercise — just see what seems to attract you, and if it feels right, include it. You may be surprised by which images call to you. (This is the subconscious making itself known.)

When you have collected all the images you need, the next step is to bring them together into a whole, perhaps by creating a collage. You'll need some posterboard, glue (maybe glitter and other decorations!), and some markers. You can also include photographs, words of encouragement or inspiration in your treasure map, and anything else that will make it meaningful to you.

When you're done, put your treasure map somewhere you will see it regularly. As you take time to see what you want to bring more of into your life, you will send out attractive energy targeted to that desire. And you will notice interesting responses as a result.

TAKING ACTION

Your life mirrors what you put into it or withhold from it. When you hold back, it holds back. When you hesitate, it stands there staring, hands in its pockets. But when you commit, it comes on like blazes.

David Bayles and Ted Orland, Art and Fear

I love this quote. It can be so hard to make the transition between wanting something and being willing to commit to it. Being clear about what we want is a vital step in creating a full color life. Now, we are ready for action.

Easier said than done, however; too often we say we want to do something, but for some reason we don't act on it. Artist Greg Mort regularly runs across people who express a desire to paint, but don't act on it:

> For years I have had the opportunity to talk to people who come to my show in Maine who say, "Boy, one of these days I'm going to get some paint." Of course they never do. Even that statement alone, I've learned, tells me

they're never going to do it. If they were going to do it, they would have already done it.

Sonia Choquette captures the difference between hopes and intentions:

> Wishes and hopes are potentially weak and can be diminished, deflected, and dashed. Intentions, on the other hand, are royal and, when they rise up from the soul, will be treated royally.[31]

Like the would-be artists Greg runs across, wishes are weak and may not take us very far. But intentions are royal; they have an attractive power all their own. So here is our opportunity to act in alignment with our intentions. Even though the outcome is not certain, by taking steps in alignment with our desires, we set events in motion, and by doing so offer an invitation to God or the universe to respond.

There is a tremendous upside to acting on our intentions. This is how we become the people we yearn to be — authentic, self-disciplined, trusting of our inner wisdom, and willing to rely on it.

Is the outcome always exactly what we expected? Of course not. We can't place an order for the future we choose, and that's a good thing, because often what emerges is better or more appropriate than we had envisioned. But we can take responsibility for taking skillful steps toward the outcome we desire.

One primary rule is to apply our intention — to take action — from our center. In other words, if you have an inner committee member that is trying to convince you that this is the job for you, but you know deep down that it isn't, pay attention. Distinguishing your true inner voice from the opinion of a loud committee member will help you avoid taking the wrong job. Action must be directly tied to that center of wisdom within. Being true to yourself brings joy.

Another primary rule is to operate from the present moment. Now here's a challenge: we are intending for something to happen, which by definition is in the future, yet we need to keep our spirit in the present moment. By aligning our actions with the present moment, we are more likely to head in a direction which is true to us and guided by spirit.

We can't live in the future, and that's a good thing. Life happens in the present moment. Things change, opportunities are presented, the landscape shifts — so we need to be here, living our lives, and directing our actions, from that place of 'now.'

So we've clarified our intentions, operated from our center, focused on living in the here and now, and taken action in support of our desires. Our final task is to let go.

See what emerges. Accept unexpected results or detours. Keep an attitude of curiosity and be free of judgments. Be open to the unfolding of your life, and flexible in your response. Life doesn't often proceed along straight lines, but if we stay present and connected, the journey can be a joyful, fascinating one.

Finally, expect good things. If in the past your steps were burdened by the common barriers we have discussed — such as unreasonable expectations, lack of self-awareness, or fear of being true to yourself — now you have challenged some of these barriers and strengthened your ability to act on your own behalf. You know in your heart that if you can find ways to be more true to yourself, your life will become more authentically self-expressive, and therefore more joyful. And at the very least, if you are true to yourself, the journey will be far more interesting!

THE DESTINATION

So what does success look like? Our culture tends to suggest it is the job, house, car, bank account, and perhaps our standing in society. As we said earlier, although we all need the basics of life, these need not define success for us.

Further, success doesn't require that every intention we have is manifested completely. We will have goals that don't pan out. Our routes will be more circuitous than expected, and may end in unintended locations.

Success as defined by our society, and a successful full color life, may look somewhat different. A successful full color life transcends our goals. Jack Weltner offers a perfect summary:

> Full color living is living increasingly transparently. That means letting my inside shine through, without worrying about looking good or getting anywhere. This becomes easier and more fun, and you are offering more of your self — spontaneity, aliveness, joy — to others.

Full color living happens when we function from the deep core of our being. It requires being content with being simply ourselves, and being willing to act on our individuality. Success is measured in the joy we bring to our lives, and to the lives of others.

Being true to yourself brings joy. I invite you to take up this rich, rewarding, full color journey, as only you can!

ABOUT THE AUTHOR

JENNIFER JOY WALKER, M.A., started out life as an actress, and has been on a fascinating journey ever since. Her mission is to inspire others to tap into their own wisdom and gifts in order to enjoy fully expressive lives.

Most recently an internal organization development consultant for Walt Disney World, Jennifer has worked over the past 20+ years with dozens of companies and hundreds of individual clients as a consultant and coach. Jennifer speaks and offers workshops and seminars on *Full Color Living, Full Color Work* and *Full Color Organizations*.

Jennifer earned a Master of Arts degree in Vocational Counseling and Spiritual Psychology from Lesley University in Cambridge, Massachusetts. She is a graduate of the Drama Studio, London. She has also written a career exploration workbook, *Full Color Work: A self-exploration and planning guide for people who want to do what they love.*

Jennifer lives on the Gulf Coast of Florida with her husband, Woody Fletcher, and their big old yellow lab, Yeller.

To contact Jennifer:
jennifer@fullcolorliving.com
www.fullcolorliving.com
(941) 388-7447

Bibliography & Resources

Bayles, David and Orland, Ted. *Art and Fear: Observations on the Perils (and Rewards) of Artmaking.* Santa Cruz, CA: Image Continuum Press, 2001.

Bellman, Geoffrey. *The Consultant's Calling: Bringing Who You Are to What You Do.* San Francisco: Jossey-Bass, 2002. (2nd edition)

Buechner, Frederick. *Wishful Thinking: A Seeker's ABC,* New York: HarperCollins Publishers, 1973

Buckingham, Marcus and Clifton, Donald O. *Now, Discover Your Strengths.* New York: The Free Press, 2001

Buckingham, Marcus. *Go Put Your Strengths to Work.* New York: Free Press, 2007

Cameron, Julia. *The Artist's Way: A Spiritual Path to Higher Creativity.* New York: Jeremy P. Tarcher, 1992

Choquette, Sonia, Ph.D. *Your Heart's Desire: Instructions for Creating the Life You Really Want.* New York: Three Rivers Press, 1997

Csikszentmihalyi, Mihaly. *Finding Flow: The Psychology of Engagement with Everyday Life.* New York: Basic Books, 1997.

Domar, Alice D. and Dreher, Henry. *Self Nurture: Learning to Care for Yourself as Effectively as You Care for Everyone Else.* New York: Penguin Books, 2000

Hicks, Esther and Jerry. *Ask and It Is Given: Learning to Manifest Your Desires.* Carlsbad, CA: Hay House, 2004.

_____.*The Amazing Power of Deliberate Intent: Living the Art of Allowing.* Carlsbad, CA: Hay House, 2006.

Housden, Roger. *Seven Sins for a Life Worth Living.* New York: Harmony Books, 2005

Jung, C.G. *The Integration of the Personality.* London: Kegan Paul, Trench, Trubner & Co. Ltd., 1940

Kabat-Zinn, Jon. *Wherever You Go There You Are.* New York: Hyperion, 1994

Knox, Deborah L. and Butzel, Sandra S. *Life Work Transition.com: Putting Your Spirit Online.* Woburn, MA, 2000.

Levoy, Gregg. *Callings: Finding and Following an Authentic Life.* New York: Three Rivers Press, 1997

Merron, Keith. *Consulting Mastery.* San Francisco: Berrett-Koehler Publishers, 2005

Myss, Caroline, Ph.D. *Anatomy of the Spirit: The seven stages of power and healing.* New York: Three Rivers Press, 1996.

Naparstek, Belleruth. *Your Sixth Sense: Activating Your Psychic Potential.* New York: HarperCollins, 1997.

O'Connor, Elizabeth. *Journey Inward, Journey Outward.* San Francisco: Harper & Row. 1968

Palmer, Parker J. *The Active Life: A Spirituality of Work, Creativity, and Caring.* San Francisco: Jossey-Bass, 1990.

_____. *Let Your Life Speak: Listening for the Voice of Vocation.* San Francisco: Jossey-Bass, 1999

Ray, Michael. *The Highest Goal: The Secret That Sustains You in Every Moment.* San Francisco: Berrett-Koehler Publishers, 2004

Ray, Michael and Myers, Rochelle. *Creativity in Business.* New York: Doubleday, 1986

Richardson, Cheryl. *Take Time For Your Life.* New York: Broadway Books, 1998.

Rinpoche, Sogyal. *The Tibetan Book of Living and Dying.* New York: Harper Collins, 1992

Sher, Barbara. *I Could Do Anything If I Only Knew What It Was.* New York: Delacorte Press, 1994

_____. *Live the Life You Love: in Ten Easy, Step-By-Step Lessons.* New York: Dell Publishing, 1996

_____. Wishcraft: *How to Get What You Really Want.* New York: Ballentine Books, 1979

Sinetar, Marsha. *Do What You Love, The Money Will Follow.* New York: Paulist Press, 1987

_____. *To Build the Life You Want, Create the Work You Love.* New York: St. Martin's Press, 1995

Talbot, Michael. *The Holographic Universe.* New York: HarperCollins, 1991

Tolle, Eckhart. *A New Earth: Awakening to Your Life's Purpose.* New York: Penguin Group, 2005

Whyte, David. *The Heart Aroused.* New York: Doubleday, 1994

Winfield, Carol L. *Yoga in the Morning, Martini at Night (or The First Three-Score and Ten are the Hardest).* 1st Books Library. 2001

References

[1] *A New Earth*, p. 59

[2] Concord Institute Training program, 1993

[3] For more information about psychosynthesis, see the website for the Association for the Advancement of Psychosynthesis: http://www.aap-psychosynthesis.org/

[4] *Consulting Mastery*, p.193

[5] *Song of the Phoenix: The Hidden Rewards of Failure*, Berkshire House Press, 1992

[6] *The Highest Goal*, p. 147

[7] *Creativity in Business*, p. 66

[8] *Wherever You Go, There You Are*, p. 11

[9] *Seven Sins for a Life Worth Living*, p. 186

[10] *Anatomy of the Spirit*, p. 216

[11] *Weavings*, May/June 1996

[12] See Jack Weltner's website, http://safe-harbor.cc, for more great insights.

[13] "Now I Become Myself." In Yes! A Journal of Positive Futures, Spring 2001

[14] *Live the Life You Love: in Ten Easy, Step-By-Step Lessons*

[15] MSNBC.Com, Rabbi Gellman: The Second Secret of Life. October 12, 2005

[16] *Go Put Your Strengths to Work* by Marcus Buckingham is an excellent resource for discovering how to do just that.

[17] *Now Discover Your Strengths*, p.8

[18] *Now Discover Your Strengths*, p. 6

[19] I first ran across this approach to discovering strengths in Richard Broholm's "Identifying Gifts and Arenas" published by the Center for the Ministry of the Laity, Newton, Massachusetts.

[20] *To Build the Life You Want, Create the Work You Love*, p. 156

[21] *Wishful Thinking: A Seeker's ABC*, p. 95

[22] *Callings: Finding and Following an Authentic Life*

[23] *Journey Inward, Journey Outward*, p.54

[24] *Take Time For Your Life*, p.24

[25] From article by Dr. Henry S. Lodge, "You can stop 'normal' aging" in Parade Magazine, March 18, 2007. He is co-author of the book, *Younger Next Year* (Workman).

[26] From his essay, "Embracing the Everyday"

[27] *The Consultant's Calling: Bringing Who You Are to What You Do*, p.68

[28] Phone interview

[29] *The Heart Aroused*, p. 11.

[30] *Simple Abundance: A Daybook of Comfort and Joy*

[31] *Your Heart's Desire: Instructions for Creating the Life You Really Want*, p. 27